Vashti's Victory

M000012143

Vashti's Victory

and Other Biblical Women Resisting Injustice

LaVerne McCain Gill

THE PILGRIM PRESS

CLEVELAND

This book is dedicated to

MARY WILLIAMS, MY MOTHER, AND CLEMENT WILLIAMS, MY STEPFATHER

DR. TEPPER L. GILL, MY HUSBAND

DYLAN MCCAIN MCDUFFIE AND TEPPER MCCAIN GILL, MY SONS

JENNETTE HARDY, MY STEPDAUGHTER

JOHN AND PAUL MCCAIN, MY BROTHERS

KYANA, RASHON, MARK, AND MARLENE MCCAIN, MY NIECES AND NEPHEWS

In loving memory of

FREDERICK MCCAIN, MY BROTHER

PAUL MCCAIN, MY FATHER

The Pilgrim Press, 700 Prospect Avenue, Cleveland, Ohio 44115-1100
pilgrimpress.com
© 2003 by LaVerne McCain Gill

Biblical quotations, unless otherwise noted, are from the New Revised Standard Version of the Bible, © 1989 by the Division of Christian Education of the National Council of Churches of Christ in the U.S.A., and are used by permission. Adaptations have been made for inclusivity.

All rights reserved. Published 2003

Printed in the United States of America on acid-free paper

08   07   06   05   04   03   5   4   3   2   1

Library of Congress Cataloging-in-Publication Data
Gill, LaVerne McCain, 1947–
     Vashti's victory and other biblical women resisting injustice /
  LaVerne McCain Gill.
         p.   cm.
     Includes bibliographical references (p.).
     ISBN 0-8298-1521-X (pbk. : alk. paper)
     1. Women in the Bible.   2. Christian women—Religious life.
  I. Title: Half title Vashti's victory.   II. Title.

BS575.G55   2003
220.9'082—dc21

                                                2003048257

Contents

Acknowledgments

How do you thank so many people who have been so supportive? Let me make an attempt. First of all I would like to give honor, praise, and thanks to God, who has given me gifts that are undeserved. Second, I would like to thank my immediate family, starting with my mother, Mary Williams, who has been a spiritual presence, a strong support, and my best friend. She models unconditional love—the kind that God so graciously gives. Clement Williams, my stepfather, has been more than a father to me and has loved and cared about me for nearly half of my adult life. As always, I want to acknowledge the love and support of my husband, Dr. Tepper Gill, who stands beside me in all of my endeavors with a gentle nudge of encouragement when times get tough.

A very special note of acknowledgement to my sons, Tepper and Dylan; they have always been my inspiration. Their spiritual quests have taught me a lot and my love for them is boundless. Paul and John, my brothers, share in this venture with me. They encourage me and support me in my writing and in my ministry.

During the writing of this book, I have had the pleasure of learning and growing in the Spirit as the pastor of Webster United Church of Christ. I owe a great deal of gratitude to that congregation for their support and love. I especially want to thank Dr. Brenda McGadney Douglass for her insight and experience in Ghana with the Trokosi women. She pointed the way to significant research on this issue.

Last, but certainly not least, Natasha Kern, my agent, and Kim Sadler, my acquiring editor, made this book possible. Thank you both.

Introduction

What's Behind the Title?

It was the day after the acquittal of O. J. Simpson.[1] As a divided nation was engaged in vitriol, I sat in a seminary class entitled "The Social Construction of Evil." It was a predominately white seminary, with most students the age of my then twenty-five-year-old son. The classroom had three African American students, the other two of whom were males, about as old as I was, give or take five or ten years. I was forty-eight.

The professor opened his lecture with the statement: "If I were a social worker in Los Angeles today, I would take all black people off of welfare." Then he proceeded to discuss the verdict and criticize the predominately African American female jurors. The two other African Americans in the class looked up from their papers and glanced across the room at each other and at me. Had we been younger, we probably would have accepted the bait that was offered up and engaged in an exchange of verbal warfare that would have triggered the debate about race and justice. Instead, we made eye contact with each other and said nothing.

Several days later the seminary had a forum on the O. J. Simpson verdict, because tensions were running high on the campus full of would-be ministers filled with emotions ranging from outrage to revenge to vindication. The lecture hall was packed, and I reluctantly joined the audience to hear what was being said. In front of the students sat three faculty members, among them the professor who had made the comment about welfare.

I decided to speak out. "I don't understand how we can talk about the racism in California when we have racism right here at the seminary that includes racial remarks being made in the classroom stemming from this verdict." There was silence, with some African American students nodding their heads. A few minutes later, I left the room.

Literally running after me and following me down the stairs was the professor.

"Were you talking about me in there?" he asked moving close to me.

"Yes, I was," I responded.

"Are you calling me a racist?" he said.

"Are you?" I responded.

"What is your name, and don't you have a paper due in my class?" he asked, while pulling out a small pad and pen from his vest jacket.

"My name is LaVerne Gill, and I hope you don't think that you can intimidate me with that question."

He wrote down my name.

"Are you accusing me of threatening you about grades?"

"I am saying to you that I am not some twenty-five-year-old student, on a scholarship, afraid of a grade. You cannot intimidate me in that way. I am a grown woman paying my own way and I don't care about grades."

"Are you accusing me of being intellectually dishonest?" he demanded.

"Are you?"

By this time other students had gathered around, standing a short distance away trying to hear what was being said. He had begun to raise his voice.

"You had better write this up if you consider it a complaint," he said.

"I am not writing up anything."

"Let me tell you something," I continued. "I don't have to like you and you don't have to like me. All you have to do is come and teach your class and all I have to do is attend, pay attention, and turn in my assignments. I don't want, nor do I need, any favors."

He stormed away and left the building.

A few days later I received a letter from the chaplain of the seminary, advising me that any communication that I needed to have with this teacher should come through him or through another female faculty member. The letter further advised me that the professor team teaching the course would be the one who would grade my final paper.

Since the course was entitled the "Social Construction of Evil," I decided that my paper would be entitled: "The Vashti Paradigm: Systemic Violence Against Women of Color Who Rebel against Patriarchal Authority." I received an A minus on the paper.

This anecdote illustrates, more than anything, the courage that one can take from the biblical stories, especially if you are a woman of color up against a system that would rather destroy you than support you. I am certain that if I had *blinked,* if I had not been able to stand my ground, in spite of the potential threat of a bad grade, if I had not known that God and not humans charted my path, I would have caved in. It was then that I found in the story of Vashti a story that could provide the sustenance that would guide me through moments like these.

I searched for other biblical stories and found that Vashti (Esth. 1, 2; Esth. (Greek/Apochryphal) 1, 2), was not alone. She is certainly the one who pointed me to other courageous biblical women of resistance against injustice, such as: Shiprah and Puah (Ex. 1:15); Jochebed (Ex. 2:1–10, 6:20; Num. 26:59); Miriam (Ex. 2:1–10, 15:20–21; Num. 12:1–15, 20:1, 26:59; Deut. 24:9; 1 Chron. 6:3; Mic. 6:4); the Pharaoh's daughter (Ex. 2:7–10); the daughters of Zelophehad (Num. 26:33, 27:1–7, 36:2–11; 1 Chron. 7:15); Michal (1 Sam. 14:49, 18:20–28, 19:11–17, 25:44; 2 Sam. 3:13–14, 6:16–23, 21:8; 1 Chron. 15:29); the woman who anoints Jesus at Bethany (Mark 14:3–9); and Susanna (Susanna, the Apocryphal/Deuterocanonical Books). For too long, these women have been considered minor characters in the history of theological reflection, preaching, and exegesis.

Their theological place in the salvation story has often been overlooked or viewed as perhaps just a literary nuance to get on with the rest of the story—the one about the men in their midst who were the real *select* of God. Traditional approaches to these women would have the reader believe that each one's role in the salvation story is derived from her relationship to a primary biblical figure such as Moses, Esther, Daniel, David, and the disciples. That is not the premise of this book. In this book—*Vashti's Victory and Other Biblical Women Resisting Injustice*—I employ the "justice reading strategy" to gain a different understanding of these women's place in God's plan for salvation.

The justice reading strategy goes beyond the narrative that directs attention to the primarily male leader and focuses on a more holistic view of the story. It is a view that seeks discernment about God's purpose in the narrative, rather than human preoccupation with heroes and heroines. The justice reading strategy—borrowed from the literary tradition—speaks to the inclusion of these women in the biblical story as integral to our understanding of how God works in the world. The justice reading strategy makes the assumption that God chose to thwart injustice through the actions of these women.

The justice reading strategy, introduced in my book, *Daughters of Dignity: African Women in the Bible and the Virtues of Black Womanhood*[2] continues to inform and enlighten my understanding of the role of women in the Bible. This installment into that interpretation once again highlights the role that women play in God's story about salvation. Patriarchy, gender, race, and class have been used in the past to point to the oppression of biblical women. This has led to the feminist and womanist perspectives that paint women as victims of a patriarchal system that overwhelms them and keeps them from being full participants in the salvation story. While such an interpretation may have been the intent of the Biblical writers and the commentators that come later, I believe that it is not the intent of a God of justice. God's call for justice is evident throughout the Bible, but nowhere more poignant and powerful than in the stories that include the women of scripture.

In other words, the intention might have been to suppress the voice of women in the Bible, but a God of justice's intention would be to create stories that show that women are a part of God's created reality, and that they resist the culture that oppresses them against God's will for their freedom. *Vashti's Victory and Other Biblical Women Resisting Injustice* shows that women do not have to wage that battle with God. God is revealed through their acts of rebellion and resistance. These biblical women evidence courage in the face of oppression and they resist efforts that attempt to thwart the movement of God in the world. Many biblical women represent pockets of resistance allowing for God's realm to break through on earth.

This image of biblical women speaks to the inner souls of the women who have stood up for God in strange places, and in strange lands. Everyone speaks about the risks of Moses, but the Pharaoh's daughter also took a risk; Shiphrah and Puah also took a risk; Jochebed and Miriam ventured into a risky effort to save Moses—God's chosen liberator of the Hebrew people. Not all of these women of courage escaped the wrath of the outside world. Vashti paid for her decision to say "no" with the loss of her status, her husband, and her home. The daughters of Zelophehad sought economic justice and God responded. Michal resisted her father Saul's attempt to kill David, but she paid for it by losing her zest for life and living. Susanna was triumphant in her resistance, but not until after losing her reputation. The woman at Bethany, ridiculed by the disciples, gained status in the eyes of Jesus as one who performed a prophetic act.

Oftentimes women's history paints resistance as a modern phenomenon. However, the resistance that women have put forth within the last couple of centuries is not new. The abolitionist, the feminist, the suffragette, and the civil rights activist were not created out of whole cloth. Rather, such fervor for justice has been in the culture of women throughout their time on earth. Traditional theologians may have labeled Eve as the cause of original sin, but she was also the mother of resistance and rebellion. Unfortunately, hers happened to be *against* God. The women in *Vashti's Victory* resisted *for* God, earning them a place in the salvation story. There have been some biblical women portrayed as less than noble in their resistance, such as Jezebel and Athalia. However, they too were rebelling for their own understanding of God to be made manifest in the land of their birth—Canaan.

Vashti's Victory looks at six biblical stories and discusses them using the justice reading strategy. The stories are given a frame of reference by an analysis of the Vashti story in the first chapter of the book. They are stories of women who rebelled against oppression in order to have God's work made manifest in the world.

The biblical women are compared with contemporary women or women of recent history who have resisted oppression of various types—economic, political, religious, cultural. For example, the resistance of women such as Ida B. Wells Barnett showed the lengths to which an unjust system in America would go to preserve the custom of lynching blacks. For her resistance, Wells Barnett was run out of Memphis, losing her home, business, and almost her life. Like Vashti, she exacted a heavy price for her resistance.

Vashti's Victory and Other Biblical Women Resisting Injustice has four major objectives:

- To give the reader new insights and new strategies for reading the Bible.

- To place this new information in the context of the history of women who have resisted oppressive social structures in order to further the reign of God on earth.

- To explore personal faith journeys through self-assessment and theological reflection. Study questions are provided following each chapter so that readers might reflect on their personal faith journeys and discern where they fit in this long line of resistance for justice.

- To open up new vistas of interpretation for men and women who read, study, and preach from the biblical stories.

In summary, *Vashti's Victory and Other Biblical Women Resisting Injustice* is for women and men who embrace the understanding of the work of God in history as one that includes all of God's created reality. It is a book that helps women to overcome the perception of victimhood that surrounds some theological thinking about women in the Bible. *Vashti's Victory and Other Biblical Women Resisting Injustice* should, if successful, create a more proactive response to the scriptural mandates for social justice.

ORGANIZATION

The book has six chapters, an introduction, and an epilogue. The sections of the book are as follows. Each chapter contains the following:

- A narrative account of a biblical story
- Comparison between the traditional commentary and the application of the justice reading strategy
- A cultural hermeneutic highlighting contemporary women or women of recent history who have resisted similar injustices
- A conclusion with reflection questions

RATIONALE

Why write *Vashti's Victory and Other Biblical Women Resisting Injustice?*

In touring with my book *Daughters of Dignity: African Women in the Bible and the Virtues of Black Womanhood,* no matter what the composition of the audience—African American, Euro-American, Hispanic, Native American—the response has consistently included those women who found in the book's stories strength for their personal faith journey. They have been able to look at women in the Bible in a different light and have been able to come closer to understanding that they are a part of God's created reality.

In many speaking engagements, I spoke not only about the women in *Daughters*—Hagar, Queen of Sheba, Rahab, the Canaanite woman, and Zipporah—but I included some of the women in this current book. I talked about women such as Vashti, whose resistance caused her to lose what some might consider everything for the sake of her dignity and self-esteem;

the five women surrounding Moses and their role in saving his life so that he might fulfill God's plan for liberation; the daughters of Zelophehad and their resistance to the economic injustice against women of the day; Susanna and her quest for justice in the midst of sexual harassment by powerful men; Michal and her rebellion against her father in an effort to save the life of David and what it cost her; and the woman who anointed Jesus at Bethany, enduring the abuse of the disciples in order to perform a prophetic act for Jesus.

These stories have proven time and again to give new insights into the Bible for many women. For some it has even given them a renewed interest in Christianity and their own faith journeys. Told repeatedly that they are not considered integral to the story of salvation, many women have fallen prey to the rhetoric and have lost interest in a religion that they perceive does not address them as having value and worth to God's salvific plan for humanity.

I do not believe that God intended for women to get that message. I think that the veil of silence can be pierced and women can read the story in a different way—one that will empower them and enhance their vision of themselves as essential to God's mission on earth.

Using the story of Vashti as a paradigm for looking at these other stories gives new opportunity for fresh exegetical work and brings "good news" to those who thought that they may have been a footnote in the biblical narrative. With this new insight, women will be able to see that God not only seeks justice for them, but also uses them in the process of fighting injustice. I believe that *Vashti's Victory and Other Biblical Women Resisting Injustice* provides such insights.

1

The Vashti Victory

Biblical Women Resisting Injustice

SCRIPTURE READINGS
Esther 1, 2:1–4
Book of Esther (Greek Apocryphal writings) 1, 2:1–4

Whenever I have an opportunity to preach to women who are incarcerated or to women who have imprisoned themselves in one way or another, I use the Vashti scripture. Each time I find new meaning in it—meaning that gives strength to women who are up against odds that seem insurmountable or are in situations that they feel are unchangeable. Vashti's story is one that says to women who have made a mistake, or women who have lost their sense of self-esteem, women who have been beaten up or beaten down, that they can change the direction of their lives by saying "no" to past oppressive situations. No matter how many times they have said "yes"—either tacitly or openly—they can change the course of their lives by saying "no."

The scripture never tells us how many times Vashti agreed to come at the whim of the king. We do not know how many times she allowed herself to be treated as property. All we know is that this time, she said "no." For women who have been incarcerated because of something they did to please a man, to gain a sense of self-esteem or to self-destruct, it is never too late to say "no" to oppression, even if it is self-imposed.

The sermon does not end there. What I also teach and preach about is that these are not easy "no's." The consequences may be great, as in the case of Vashti, who lost everything—her husband, her home, her status. We can assume that the situation had come to the point where the only thing that mattered was her dignity. The time had come to shift gears and begin to value the person that God created. That is the empowering message in Vashti's story. The time had come to be a "pocket of resistance" to personal injustice. Few people get a chance to look at Vashti's story. Most rush to Esther, bypassing this powerful story of resistance.

The book of Esther was a late addition to the Old Testament. Some scholars believe that the lack of a clear presence of God in the narrative led to its late inclusion in the scriptures. The book, nevertheless, made it into the final Bible and with it the opening story about Vashti's response to the king. In looking at the divinely inspired Word of the Bible, it is possible to find that the lesson in the Vashti story comes as God speaks through Vashti's reaction to the king. Her response to the king shows that she no longer sees herself as the property of a man, but as a child of God. Her "no" speaks to all of us—saying that we have a chance to change oppressive situations at any time in order to become what God would have us be.

A good contemporary example of this lesson is a teen television program that I produced some years ago where a dynamic health educator spoke to the young people, challenging those who had been sexually active to become "virgins again." She told them that they may have had sex in the past, that they may have even become pregnant and had a child, but she proclaimed, "You can become a virgin again, by just saying 'no.'" It was a provocative statement at that time or any time. But the point is not lost on those who may have thought that the way things were, was the way things had to be. This thought that maybe they might be able to reverse the course of their lives by taking control of the person that God created was a revelation for many. There were risks. They could lose friends, boyfriends, and social acceptance among their peers, but they would gain their self-respect and use God's gift of creation to God's glory. That was the challenge. It is also the challenge inherent in looking into Vashti's victory.

These anecdotes point to the ways in which the story of Vashti comes alive and serves as a model—a paradigm for justified resistance against individual oppression. In this chapter, the story of Vashti will be analyzed in terms of its biblical status in the book of Esther, traditional commentaries about the scripture, and the manner in which the justice reading strategy may be used to gain a deeper understanding of Vashti's role in the salvation story. This chapter concludes with questions after a segment about Ghana, West Africa, where women are in situations where a Vashti victory could change the course of their lives.

RETELLING THE NARRATIVE

The book of Esther is made up of two stories that may have their origins in two different cultures—the story of the intrigue surrounding Vashti and her disobedience to the king and the story of Mordecai and Esther's heroism in saving the Jews from a threat of genocide. It is no wonder, then, that the book itself has been criticized for not including remnants of the Jewish law as evidenced in other books within the Hebrew Bible. All of these historical doubts notwithstanding, Esther has become a favorite book for many women who champion her actions; however, few have taken time out to look at the story of Vashti. Fewer still have used her as a prism through which to view biblical women and their role in the salvation story of God.

Vashti, the queen who preceded Esther, could easily be called a scapegoat or, as some commentators have said, a "comedic relief" leading up to the serious story of Esther. Such dismissive descriptions of the story tend to minimize the significance of the scripture. The story of Vashti begins with two celebrations in the palace. The first one is being held by King Ahasuerus.[1] In the third year of his reign, he gave a party for all of his officials and ministers; the army of Persia and Media and the nobles and governors of the provinces were present. The party had been going on for one hundred and eighty days. The king then gave a seven-day banquet for the people of Susa. This extravagant party included drinks that were served in goblets of different kinds. Drinking was "without restraint."

While the king's party was going on, Queen Vashti, his Persian wife, was holding a banquet for the women at the palace. After the last seven days of drinking, the king called his eunuchs in and told them to summon Vashti and have her come in wearing the royal crown while showing off her beauty. Queen Vashti refused to come at the king's command. The king became enraged and consulted his legal officials about what should be done when a queen disobeys the king. The counsel told the king that Queen Vashti had not only disobeyed him, but had caused harm to the kingdom, because other women would think that they, too, could disobey their husbands. The eunuchs warned that the women would rebel against the king's officials, and there would be chaos in the kingdom. The eunuchs advised the king to send an edict out throughout the provinces that required all women to obey their husbands, and to let all know that Queen Vashti could not come before the king ever again. The letters sent out said that every man should be "master in his own house." It was following this edict that the king began seeking out virgins, resulting in Esther replacing Vashti as queen.

TRADITIONAL COMMENTARIES ON THE STORY

The society against which the story of Purim is enacted can be summed up in one word: degenerate. It is the Persian courtly and aristocratic fraternity, which finds its delight in drunken orgies, in gastronomic feats of 180 days' duration, followed by another banquet of seven days' duration, to which all the citizens of Shushan were invited. . . . In that debauched society, sanity was suspended and marital relationships compromised.[2]

Many scholars believe that the story of Esther is a blend of historical fact and fiction—perhaps contributing to the reason why the book of Esther was not initially readily accepted into the Hebrew Bible. Another reason that Esther is different is that the story does not mention the name of God or discuss directly the Hebrew history of deliverance from Egypt.

One commentator put it this way:

The book of Esther has been the subject of critical and literary analysis by Bible scholars almost as much as any other text in the Bible. Aside from the question of the historicity of the events it relates, a great deal of attention has been given to the structure of Esther as a narrative. One comes to the conclusion that the author of this story was a writer of considerable literary talents.[3]

Some see it as a narrative whose only purpose is to establish the Hebrew tradition of Purim. Others believe that it speaks to an unspecified time when Jews were threatened with genocide. The threat was thwarted by the courageous action of Esther, a Jewess, who had hidden her religious identity to become the queen of Persia. Historians have not been able to trace the veracity of the events that unfold in Esther. They have, however, been able to tie the period to the reign of Xerxes I (486–465 B.C.E.), the Persian king called Ahasuerus in Esther and Artaxerxes in the Greek version of the story. While there is no indication that there was a Jewish queen, there is an indication that Vashti could very well have been Amestris, a Persian who was queen to Xerxes I during that time.[4]

Susa, the location of the lavish party, was the place where Xerxes I had a residence. Xerxes I did rule the Persian Empire, which at the time spanned the areas from India to Ethiopia. These were subdivided into provinces. Additional historical findings point to excavations that have been uncovered, revealing the remnants of a lavish lifestyle that took place in the courts of Susa.

Whether fact or fiction, Vashti has intrigued both Jewish and Christian scholars, as does the book of Esther in general. Lauded for its narrative aesthetic, the book is unique in the Old Testament Hebraic sacred literature, where it stands as a reminder of the nationalistic attempts of the writers to establish a basis for the sacred festival of Purim. In so doing, it prefaces its story line with a narrative that begins with the deposing of a disobedient queen, some say as a literary device for imparting the rest of the story. The book of Esther is one of the few books in the Bible that evokes strong criticism for its ethical tone, while also earning praise for its aesthetic narrative style.

Traditional commentary generally elevates the actions of Esther to a level of heroism. They point to Esther's response to Mordecai's call for her to use her position as queen—"After that I will go to the King . . . and if I perish, I perish." (Esth. 4:16). For these commentators, the book of Esther is largely the story of the threat of genocide against the Jews that was thwarted by her bold actions of confronting the king about the impending danger. Criticism that focuses primarily on the encounter of Esther with the king generally lacks any ethical considerations regarding the violence instigated by Esther and Mordecai. Rather, it tends to justify the violence, speak of Esther's heroism, and ignore her personal frailties of duplicity and deception.

When ethical critiques are provided, they tend to focus on the actions of Mordecai. Commentators in such instances might note that the story of Esther, the Jewess who is given to the Persian King Ahasuerus, is a story of the misuse of women for national aims and religious acceptance. Commentary of this nature might note that not only is Esther stripped of her virginity as a young woman, but she is also stripped of her identity as a Jew. All of this is done in order to further the desire of her uncle Mordecai to gain proximity to power.

Vashti, on the other hand, has not fared well in Jewish commentary at all. For the most part, she is looked upon as the queen who made way for Esther—a scapegoat, perhaps, as defined by the scholar René Girard. In his book *Job the Victim of his People,* Girard describes the scapegoat as "the innocent party who polarizes a universal hatred."[5] He further states that:

> The obligatory inevitably prevails over the forbidden, since there is only one concern in ritual . . . the upholding of public order and the prevention of uncontrollable chaos. The fact that the scapegoat's crimes tend to become initiation tests or even, ultimately, acts of bravado does not permit us to doubt the initially criminal character of the required deeds . . . the former crimes of the scapegoat have become coronation rites. Thus ritual imitation gives birth to significant reforms.[6]

Very few scholars have gone so far as to label Vashti a scapegoat; perhaps that is because they have not given serious thought to her story. Using Girard's definition, Vashti could be looked upon as the scapegoat that gave the king a reason for tightening the reigns on women in the kingdom. She could be considered a scapegoat who made way for the king to get another wife. She could also be considered the one who initiated the reforms that followed, even though they were oppressive to the women of the provinces.

The mere fact that Vashti was entertaining the women in her own quarters showed that she enjoyed a reputation that placed her in a position of power in the king's domain—a power that would not last long. Her defiant act gave the king and the king's advisors an opportunity to exert their power over her and the rest of the women in the provinces. In short order after her defiant act, she became the pariah of the provinces, banished from the palace and demonized by commentaries in the centuries that followed. Although her "criminal" act against Ahasuerus was really a response to her own exploitation, very little theological attention is given to her story. The contemporary interpretation of her actions in a womanist-conscious reading—where empowerment of women to overcome repressive conditions is valued as a way of witnessing God's work in the world against injustice—makes her a heroine, more so than Esther.

Commentator Jeffrey Cohen has acknowledged this admirable character trait in Vashti:

> Queen Vashti . . . must have been a rare woman to have retained her sense of dignity and morality to the extent that she was prepared to endanger her life by refusing her lord and master's bidding to show off her body to the assembled throng.[7]

Cohen goes on to say:

> It has to be said that Vashti gets a terrible press in the Midrash. This is not surprising since she was presented as the granddaughter of King Nebuchadnezzar, who took the Jews into captivity in Babylon.[8]

Cohen's commentary speaks to one of the interpretations found in Louis Ginzberg's book, *The Legends of the Jews.* In it he recounts one of the convoluted tales about Vashti. In this account, the reason for Vashti's refusal, the cause of her downfall, and the justification for her fate all centered around the destruction of the Jewish temple. In Ginzberg's retelling of the account, Vashti was not Persian but Chaldean, the daughter of Belshazzar, the son of Nebuchadnezzar, and "the one who scoffed at kings and unto whom princes were a derision."[9]

In the commentary, Vashti's fate as a queen in Ahasuerus' court is the consequence of the demise of her father's kingdom. Further, she is painted as a vain woman who refuses to come before the king unadorned because she has just given birth to a child and her body is less than perfect.

> Why, it is for thine own sake that I refuse to heed thy order. Either the people will decide that I do not come up to thy description of me and will proclaim thee a liar, or, bewitched by my beauty, they will kill thee in order to gain possession of me, saying, 'Shall this fool be the master of so much beauty?'[10]

As is evident, where womanist Christian commentary attributes a noble response to Vashti, Jewish literature demonizes her in an effort to make her fate much more acceptable in the mind of the reader. There she is not only stripped of her title and her place in the kingdom, but she is also put to death for her transgressions, which lead to a disruption in the provinces.

9

> The execution of Vashti brought most disastrous consequences in its train. His whole empire, which is tantamount to saying the whole world, rose against Ahasuerus. The widespread rebellion was put down only after his marriage with Esther, but not before it had inflicted upon him the loss of one hundred and twenty-seven provinces, the half of his kingdom. Such was his punishment for refusing permission to rebuild the temple.[11]

Even though the story of Vashti has become visible to many women as a story of triumph over oppression, the contemporary commentaries still discount her presence in the scripture. For example, *Harper's Bible Commentary* provides the following interpretation:

> A feminist read of the narrative is today inescapable, but the author more probably intends a satire against Persian men as incapable of commanding their wives' obedience. It is hardly to the credit of this absolute monarch, fabulously wealthy and masterfully supreme in every sphere, that on the domestic front he can be so decisively worsted. He, rather than Vashti, has become the spectacle.
>
> Vashti's unelaborated refusal forms an amusing contrast to the histrionic reaction of the king and his counselors. While the outcome is (perhaps) tragic for Vashti, though we observe that her punishment, never to come again before the king, is conceivably her dearest wish, is in other respects pure farce. It involves the whole elaborate machinery of Persian law and administration to say nothing of the postal service in asserting the right of every man in the empire to be master in his own house. And it is implied that the story of Vashti's independence will spread like wildfire throughout Persian lands, every wife in the empire waiting only for this sign from the empress to break out in long-stifled rebellion against her husband.[12]

Clearly, the absence of more descriptive historical information has not kept biblical scholars from addressing Ahasuerus' actions toward Vashti. In the aforementioned critique, *Harper's Bible Commentary* discounts the significance of Vashti's actions with respect to the ethical and moral underpinnings of the scripture, leaving the following question to be raised: Does Vashti play a role in God's story of salvation?

THE JUSTICE READING STRATEGY

> The one person against whom no criticism at all could be raised was Vashti, a woman of true courage and valor. While Esther vacillated before undertaking moral action, and had to be persuaded to stand up for her people, Vashti acted decisively as a moral exemplar of the highest order.[13]

The justice reading strategy speaks to the role that an obscure character in the Bible plays in the unveiling of another glimpse of God's plan for salvation. Looking for Vashti in God's plan for salvation can be difficult to discern, but not impossible.

Whatever is not known about Vashti is speculative, but what is known is instructive. She refused the summoning of the king; he reacted with the whole force of his authority against her and the rest of the women in his empire. Without speaking a word in the scripture, Vashti commands a great deal of attention by choosing self-respect over obedience to an unjust request. This view of biblical women speaks to a resistance to personal injustice that provides a model for interpreting other biblical women. What it suggests is that the plight of Vashti may be useful as a prism through which to expand our understanding of biblical women. It also addresses the issue of women who are still controlled by patriarchal customs and cultures in our contemporary societies.

Using the justice reading strategy to interpret the Vashti scripture raises the following questions: What role does Vashti play in the unfolding of God's plan for salvation? How does Vashti's story further our understanding of God's work in the world? Investigating these questions reveals an overarching problem: God is not mentioned in these scriptures. This is remedied by the writers of the Apocryphal (Greek) version of the story of Esther. The lack of a mention of God, however, does not make a theological analysis of the story prohibitive.

Despite such a major missing link, the story was able to obtain canonical status. Its mere presence in the Bible offers an opportunity to analyze it in light of God's redemptive plan for humanity. As mentioned before, neither the historicity of the story nor lack thereof has kept commentators from interpreting the actions of characters or assigning actual theological meaning to the text. Unlike Esther, though, there is some historical possibility that the character of Vashti existed—if not the incident that is described.

The role of Vashti in the story has come under recent scrutiny in Christian commentary, because her actions give rise to a different characterization of biblical women. She has become a new paradigm for biblical women. Whereas, in the past she may have been overlooked, as the strict literalist gave credence to the heroic actions of Esther, today it is Vashti's time to give definition to biblical women seeking justice and shunning oppression. Such resistance is generally associated with God's call for justice and directly speaks to the role that women play in God's unfolding plan for humanity. As a biblical text, it is a sure vehicle for giving some frame of reference for interpreting human actions and postulating theological themes.

God's call for justice and release of captives echoes throughout the Bible as God's paramount vision for all of humanity. Vashti's refusal to come at Ahasuerus' command may not have direct theological implications, but it does have a liberative theme. Vashti models what we know as God's call to resist oppression. In Vashti's reaction to the king, there is a message that speaks to the freedom of one who may have been responding to personal bondage out of brokenness. What God calls all of God's creation to is wholeness and spiritual and physical liberation. Vashti creates a different sense of personal resistance in what must have been an ordinary occurrence. Some have speculated that perhaps her meeting with the women of the province gave her a strength that she had never had before, out of which she received enough self-respect to act boldly.

A justice reading strategy sees in the Vashti scripture a model for responding to demands on one's humanity outside of the realm of God's call. Vashti gives an example of what it means to be able to say "no" to oppression and to have faith enough to accept the consequences. It is within this context that Vashti models what women can do to resist injustice. Vashti's actions are singular, but they speak to larger issues of the ability of women to respond to injustice and to accept the consequences of their actions.

THE NEW MODEL: THE VASHTI PARADIGM

Paradigm: any example or model. Latin: *paradigma,* Greek *paradeigma*—model, to compare, exhibit, alongside to show. (*The American Heritage Dictionary of the English Language*)

After reviewing the commentary on Vashti and interpreting her story using the justice reading strategy, it is now time to look at the Vashti paradigm—a new model for interpreting biblical women. If a name were to be given to the manner in which biblical women are modeled, it could easily be called the "Hagar paradigm." In this model women are viewed as being the victims of an oppressive culture—whether Hebrew or early Palestinian—or the victims of patriarchal systems reflected in the recording of the biblical witness in patriarchal terms. The result is that women are constantly viewing the Bible with skepticism.

This means that they are looking at the story, recognizing that the cultural context for women is one of unequal treatment and victimhood, and concluding that women are forgotten, oppressed, or demeaned in some way. The writing that results from such thinking keeps women questioning their role in the story of God's salvation. These writers generally cling to the stories of Deborah or Esther as ones that show them as being empowered to fight the battles that men fight. They lament the fact that many women are not named in the scriptures. They are disturbed that characterizations of women often fall into the category of "whores," "harlots," "adulteresses," or "prostitutes."

All of this might be true in terms of the writing that appears in the Bible. But in order to believe in the God of the Bible—who cares about creation—it is necessary to look beyond the human injustices of patriarchy and the human sin of sexism. Rather, one must look at how God uses all of God's creation, and most especially women, to bring about God's realm of justice, peace, and love. The walls of the society can be penetrated as well as the underlying meaning of the writing, and once that is done—if we believe that God is a God of justice—it must be assumed that women are integral to God's redemptive plans.

The Vashti paradigm is a model for women to begin to say "no" to the human bias in the writing and "yes" to God's intention for them to be a part of God's unfolding story of salvation, through their everyday acts of resistance against injustice. Consequently, the Vashti paradigm is a model for looking at other biblical women who have said "no" to different forms of injustice.

This book uses the model of Vashti to look at the daughters of Zelophehad, who said "no" to the economic disparity in the parceling out of the promised land. They said "no" and Yahweh agreed. The women surrounding Moses in his early infancy and his childhood are women who said "no" to an edict of genocide of all young Hebrew baby boys. Susanna said "no" to the sexual advances of the corrupt elders; Michal said "no" to her father, Saul, when he was trying to kill David, God's anointed. In her silence, the woman who anointed Jesus at Bethany said "no" to the disciples who ridiculed her for performing such a prophetic act for Jesus. These women fit the model of Vashti. They are not victims, but women who have been used by God to speak to the injustices of the day or to give a prophetic message for the future. They are an integral part of God's plan for salvation—from saving God's chosen leaders to exposing religious corruption. These biblical women are not mere "footnotes" in the biblical story, but significant parts of that story as it unfolds to show us a glimpse of God's presence on earth.

The following chapters will include these stories from the Bible. The next question to ask then is how does the Vashti paradigm speak to contemporary women worldwide? For many Western women, patriarchy is a matter of public discussion and debate, but in other cultures, it is still as oppressive as in the world in which Vashti existed. Take for example the following incident that occurred during this century in a small village in Ghana, West Africa.

In Ghana, you might say that there are two systems of government—the elected government and the chieftains. One could easily be called the political government and the other the cultural government. It is within the cultural government that women find themselves trapped in a patriarchal society from which they are unable to deliver themselves. While Ghana's political government and the enlightened women within it understand the nature of patriarchy and limited opportunities, they nonetheless are able to fight the laws that keep women from full access to the society. Many of these women are some of the most progressive in the world. They are educated, prolific writers, chroniclers of their stories, leaders, and theologians. But it is within the cultural government that problems exist for women. Many of these women are unable to exercise their God-given right to say "no" to oppression.

One such group of women is called the *Trokosi,* a word that means "slaves to the gods." Trokosi can be as young as five years old. Part of cultural religious practice found among the Ewe peoples of the Upper Volta region of Ghana as well as in Benin, Togo, and Nigeria, Trokosi are considered sacrifices of atonement to the gods for the alleged misdeeds of members of the family.

For example, if a relative, an ancestor, or someone within the family commits a crime—no matter how great or how small—the price for that crime is to give the next female child to the priest as an atonement or sacrifice for the sin. The girl becomes the property of the priest for as long as the sentence lasts—sometimes up to five years, other times for the rest of her life.

Menstruation is the turning point for the young Trokosi girl. Once she begins menstruating, not only is she required to work in the fields or pander in the marketplace, but she is required to have sex with the priest. If she becomes pregnant, she is responsible for the economic well-being of the child. In the event of her death or escape, her family continues to pay off the debt with the next female child.

According to the Human Rights Watch, in 1995 the Ghanaian Commission on Human Rights and Administrative Justice (CHRAJ) started a project to abolish the practice of Trokosi. At that time it was estimated that there were 3,500 girls and women bound to various shrines in the Trokosi system. This is exclusive of slave children. In 1998, the Ghanaian Government outlawed the practice of Trokosi. Half a decade later the practice was still going on, without any arrest being made. Ghana also signed the United Nations Treaty against discrimination against girls and women, but still did not get rid of the practice. The "no" response has come largely from the Non-Governmental Organizations (NGOs) and international and religious organizations. Liberation plans have been developed that would purchase the freedom of the girls (for as little as two hundred dollars) and schools have been established to train them in trades that could provide a living wage for them. Many do not marry because of the stigma attached to having been a Trokosi. It is estimated that Trokosi number in the thousands in Ghana, with even more in Benin and Togo.

ONE WOMAN SAYS "NO"

In 1999, Julie Dogbadzi, a former Trokosi from Ghana, received the Reebok Human Rights award for her efforts to fight the practice of Trokosi in Ghana. Dogbadzi knew her subject matter. At seven years of age she was handed over to the village priest as an atonement for the "sins" of a family member. It took her fourteen years to escape. She found refuge in the Ghanaian offices of an international Christian missionary and relief group. She had two children. Dognbadzi told a *Newsweek,* Atlantic reporter:

> Once, when I was three months pregnant, I decided to go to the farm and get a cob of corn. The priest caught me and got angry. He asked three other men to hold me down and . . . they put ropes on my feet, legs, and hands, and I was beaten mercilessly. . . . I was weak afterwards and almost dying. I resolved from that pain that there was no way to stay in the shrine. One day later I escaped through the bush.[14]

When the question is asked whether this book has relevance for women outside of America, the plight of the Trokosi women of Ghana answers the question in the affirmative. Perhaps it is a way of keeping the Vashti paradigm in the forefront of Christian countries with patriarchal cultures. Perhaps other women may be able to see in the story a way to say "no" to systems that are life denying, to say "no" to the prevalent specter of domestic violence, to say "no" to AIDS death sentences in their own homes, and to say "no" to female circumcision and mutilation. I believe this model is needed in a lot of places. Perhaps the women of Ghana and other developing countries where women suffer under oppressive patriarchal systems will read this story in a different way. Perhaps women will learn about the possibility of being empowered to say "no" to oppression and "yes" to liberation to live as God would have them live—to their fullest.

If a new interpretation of the Bible can provide a liberating spirit in a Christian country such as Ghana—freeing its women and men from the patriarchal interpretation of scripture and offering them a new attitude toward equality between men and women—then perhaps the Trokosi crimes will be punished and the women freed. If a holistic response to the scriptures offered something more than the model of victim-hood and oppression of women, perhaps the nature of these types of cultural mores that oppress women might change. The call for a more abundant life is meant for all of God's creation—not just men or Western women—but all of God's creation. This is the foundation upon which the Vashti paradigm rests. By using scripture to reinterpret the message of justice and liberation given to us as God's legacy for humanity, we are able to see new vistas for God's realm on earth.

THEOLOGICAL REFLECTION AND QUESTIONS

1. The prison population of women in the United States is growing at a faster rate than that of men. Many women are incarcerated for crimes that are related to bad relationships, drugs, and low self-esteem. Many have given up on religion. How would you prepare a Bible study for women in prison using the Vashti scripture?

2. Where do you see yourself in the story of Vashti? Are you in the middle of something that is keeping you from experiencing God's total glory in your life? What would it take for you to say "no" to a destructive situation to which you keep saying "yes"?

3. How would you compare the survival strategies of Vashti and Esther?

4. Fannie Lou Hamer, the noted civil rights leader, is famous for her saying "I am sick and tired of being sick and tired." Are there places in your life where you feel this way? If so, what steps have you taken to say "no"?

5. List three other biblical women who fit the Vashti paradigm. What role do you feel that they play in God's plan for salvation?

2

The Moses Event

The Women Surrounding Moses' Birth and Childhood

SCRIPTURE READINGS
Shiphrah and Puah: Exodus 1:15–22
Jochebed: Exodus 2:1–10, 6:20; Numbers 26:59
Miriam: Exodus 2:1–10, 15:20–21; Numbers 12:1–15, 20:1, 26:59;
   Deuteronomy 24:9; 1 Chronicles 6:3; Micah 6:4
The Pharaoh's daughter: Exodus 2:7–10

 The issue of attempted genocide is one of the human sins that thrive in an atmosphere of fear of the "other." Whether that other is another race, another ethnic group, or another religion or tribe, the killing of the males seems to be a major component of such human devastation. The divine providence of God is sometimes difficult to discern when such inhumane treatment is witnessed or experienced. This was the situation during the time of Moses' birth. The scripture tells us that the Pharaoh was one who did not know Joseph and feared that the Israelites were too plentiful—so plentiful that if a war were to break out they could not be able to be counted upon to be loyal to Egypt.

While conventional history assumed that the Pharaoh in question was Rameses II, more recent scholarship by the controversial Egyptologist and ancient historian David Rohl has identified the Pharaoh as Palmanothes, from ancient historians who had studied the work of Artapanus, a Jewish historian: "Artapanus writes that a pharaoh named Palmanothes was persecuting the Israelites."[1]

Although the Pharaoh made the labor of the Israelites unbearable, the oppression was not enough to assuage his fear. He needed to do more. He decided to limit the population growth by killing the male infants. Facing oppression, the Israelites cried out to God and God heard them.

God came in an unexpected way, using a diverse collection of women who came together to fulfill God's liberation plan. This intergenerational, interfaith, interracial group of women came together, creating the "Moses event." They were an unlikely alliance. The Moses event brought together women across lines of race, class, age, religion, and nationality in an effort to make God's plan for liberation manifest on earth. It is a wonderful story that begins with the resistance of two nurse midwives and ends with the actions of the Pharaoh's daughter, who chose compassion over obedience to her father.

This chapter will look at the story of the women surrounding the birth and childhood of Moses. Each in her own way became a part of God's salvific plan to raise up from among the Hebrews a liberator. Shiphrah and Puah, the nurse midwives, refused to kill Hebrew children. Jochebed and Miriam refused to let Moses die or be killed by Pharaoh. The Pharaoh's daughter went against her father's mandate and took in the Hebrew male baby boy and named him Moses. This journey from near infanticide to adoption by Pharaoh's daughter constitutes what is being called the Moses event.

RETELLING THE NARRATIVE

At the time of the birth of Moses, a Pharaoh of Egypt (who is unnamed in the scripture) is said to have felt threatened by the growth of the Hebrew population. This Pharaoh did not know the history of Joseph's special status in Egypt resulting from his good work and God's favor. Consequently, the plight of the Hebrews had worsened with their increase in numbers. Subjugated and oppressed by hard labor, they were now facing genocide at the hands of the Egyptian government. It was speculated by historians that Moses was born during the time that the Egyptian kingdom was in a decline. Pharaoh had reason to fear the invasion of the Hyskos, an Asiatic people, who later succeeded in ruling Egypt for over two hundred years.[2]

One way of controlling the increase of the Hebrews was to kill off the male offspring, since the Egyptians believed that the father of the child in this patrilineal society carried the racial lineage; the cultural/national identity of the mother did not matter. Women without men could be used as concubines and any children that resulted from these unions would be culturally compromised as interracial offspring. This is why Pharaoh told the midwives to kill the boys, but let the girls live. His attempts at infanticide were complicated because the Israelites were plentiful and fruitful, just as God had promised.

Shiphrah and Puah, two nurse midwives who tended to the births of the Hebrew women, refused to kill the babies. When questioned by Pharaoh about their disobedience, one midwife responded that the Hebrew women gave birth faster than the Egyptians before the midwives arrived, making it impossible for them to catch the babies at birth and kill them. The scripture tells us, however, that the midwives "feared God" and that is why they did not commit the murders of the Hebrew babies. Without the help of the midwives, Pharaoh had to change his strategy to a more nefarious one. He commanded that all male children be drowned in the Nile River.

Whether Shiphrah and Puah were midwives for Moses, it is not known, but the account of their acts of resistance allowed for the story of Moses to unfold in a plausible way. For three months, Moses, one of the babies spared the fate of death at birth, is kept hidden by his mother, Jochebed. Jochebed was born into the house of Levi in Egypt and her husband was Amram. They had three children—Aaron, Moses, and Miriam. (Num. 26:57–62). Although she is not named in this scripture, it is commonly assumed that Miriam is the older sister who is helping Jochebed to save Moses. Aaron is not mentioned in this scripture; therefore, it is unknown how he escaped the edict of Pharaoh.

Unable to keep him any longer, Jochebed and her daughter prepared a basket reinforced with bitumen and pitch, placed the baby in it, and situated it on the bank of the river among the reeds. Miriam watched from a distance to see what would happen to the baby. As Pharaoh's daughter was bathing, she noticed the basket in the reeds and summoned her attendants to go and get it. When she opened the basket, she saw the crying baby. She took pity on him and said, "This must be one of the Hebrews' children" (Ex. 2:6).

Miriam, who was close by, asked whether she should go and find a Hebrew nursemaid for the baby. When Pharaoh's daughter agreed, Miriam brought her mother to Pharaoh's daughter. Pharaoh's daughter then handed the baby back to his mother, Jochebed, who nursed him until he grew up. When she returned the weaned child, Pharaoh's daughter named him Moses.

Of the five women in the Moses event, Miriam is the only one whose story continues in the Mosaic narrative. Her role is expanded to include that of cocelebrant at the time of the liberation from Egypt. In Exodus 15:20–21, where she is described as a prophetess, we read about her singing and dancing in celebration of God's deliverance of the Hebrews from bondage. In Numbers 12:11–15 she challenges Moses in the wilderness. As a strict adherent to the Levite tradition of endogamy or interclan marriage, Miriam rebukes Moses for marrying a Cushite (Ethiopian) woman, and as a prophetess, she challenges his connection to God as God's exclusive messenger. For these questions and challenges to Moses, she is punished by God and turned into a ritually unclean leper. Moses intercedes with God on her behalf to reduce God's harsh sentence against her. Although both Miriam and Aaron challenge Moses, it is only Miriam who is punished so severely by God. In Numbers 20:1 we read that Miriam died in the wilderness of Zin in Kadesh and was buried there.

TRADITIONAL COMMENTARY

It was probably the Joseph tribes that took part in the Exodus, although elements of the tribe of Levi were also in Egypt. . . . Aspects of this story are paralleled in the legends of other national heroes, e.g. Sargon of Agade (about 2600 B.C.), who in infancy was saved from danger by being put in a basket of rushes sealed with pitch and floated on the river.[3]

The early life of Moses has been studied and analyzed by many religious historians. Most come to the conclusion that the story may be a combination of truth and myth. This is sometimes substantiated by the presence of a heroic "motif" that can be found in the stories of the ancient Near East and in Greek mythology.

Moshe's (Moses') birth narrative parallels that of King Sargon of Akkad; his flight from Egypt and return as leader are reminiscent of Jephthah and David in the Bible and the Syrian king Idrimi (as recounted in Akkadian texts), as well. In addition, half a century ago Lord Raglan attempted to demonstrate common elements in hero biographies by compiling a list of up to thirty key motifs. Those relevant to Moshe include: the father a relative of the mother, an attempt made to kill him at birth, his escape through the action of others, being raised by foster parents, little information about his childhood, his traveling to his "future kingdom" upon reaching adult hood, promulgating laws, losing favor with the deity, dying on the top of a hill, not being succeeded by his children, and a hazy death burial.[4]

Even though it is possible that his story might have parallels in other Near Eastern cultures, none has achieved the status and the theological significance that Moses commands on the world stage. It is a story that has survived the test of time and has gone down through the ages as the historical and theological foundation for the Judeo-Christian tradition. Recorded through divinely inspired writing and used as an inspirational and spiritual bulwark for centuries of believers, Moses' story is critical to an understanding of the Christian faith.

As mentioned previously, one historian has gone on to search for the "historical Moses" and as a consequence has discovered some compelling and controversial timelines that identify a new chronology of events. In David Rohl's research it is speculated that Moses was taken in by the daughter of a Pharaoh and later became a leader in the Egyptian army, invading Ethiopia:

> Josephus in his *Antiquities of the Jews,* with access to very old manuscripts and writing in A.D. 93, also mentioned Moses' Ethiopian or Kushite war. Here, Moses led an Egyptian army down the Nile valley, past the Third Cataract, deep into Kush (modern Ethiopia). In the British Museum is a stela that tells of a 13th Dynasty pharaoh undertaking a campaign south into the region of Kush. That pharaoh is none other than Khaneferre, the stepfather of Moses according to Artapanus. He is the only 13th Dynasty pharaoh who is recorded as having campaigned into Upper Nubia or Ethiopia.[5]

The Rohl research was conducted to establish a chronology that would prove the historical existence of Moses and re-order the commonly held notions about the timeline of that history. The value of the Rohl research to the commentary on the subject scripture is that it sheds new light on the women of the Moses event, especially the identification of the Pharaoh's daughter.

While this section focuses on the women surrounding Moses at birth, another woman also saved his life before he returned to Egypt to liberate the Hebrews. The survival motif is found again in his later life when his Midianite wife, Zipporah, saves his life as he begins his journey back to Egypt (Ex. 4:24–26). Her action, however, was an act of love, not of resistance.

The story of the nurse midwives and the various stories about Miriam have probably been given more focus by traditional scholars than any about Pharaoh's daughter or Jochebed, Moses' mother. Lauded for their act of heroism, Shiphrah and Puah have become symbols of women who held a significant role in God's salvific plan by defying Pharaoh's orders. Miriam is probably most famous for her strategy for ensuring that Jochebed was able to save Moses' life and later become his nursemaid. Each one of these women is usually considered on her own in the commentaries. Few commentators attempt to look at the group of them as a pocket of resistance to injustice on behalf of God's plan for liberation.

One exception, however, can be found in the commentary of Everett Fox:

> A natural plan of attack, to stem the human tide, is genocide. Ironically, because of his fear of war Pharaoh concentrates his worries around the males, ignoring the true source of fecundity. And it is the women in these chapters, as many commentators have pointed out . . . who play the major role in beginning the lib-

eration process. The midwives accomplish a successful cover-up; Moshe's mother and sister, and Pharaoh's daughter, save the future liberator's life. "If she be a daughter, she may live" (v.16), along with four other occurrences of "live" in vv. 17–22, underscore the irony and the certainty of Israelite survival. The use of women—a group that was often powerless in ancient societies—in these stories makes the eventual victory of the Israelites all the more striking from a traditional patriarchal point of view; the motif returns a number of times in Israelite literature, as with Jael and Judith.[6]

Not all commentators are as thorough as Fox in their discussion of the birth narrative of Moses. Thomas Mann gives short shrift to the story, while still acknowledging it as significant.

In the midst of this desperate situation—but with no explanation of its significance—a Hebrew child is born and given the name of Moses. Ironically, Pharaoh's own daughter, who unknowingly gives him to his real mother to be nursed, rescues him from Pharaoh's decree. The actions of these two women, along with those of Moses' sister and the Hebrew midwives of chapter 1, represent the only resistance to Pharaoh's villainy so far in the story.[7]

The following sections will look at the women individually and then present their stories as an involuntary collaborative effort that resulted in God's will being made manifest in the world—the Moses event.

Shiphrah and Puah

"But the midwives feared God; they did not do as the king of Egypt commanded them, but they let the boys live." (Ex. 1:17)

"In the refusal of women to cooperate with oppression, the liberation of Israel from Egyptian bondage has its beginning."[8]

The Hebrew language is not clear as to whether Shiphrah and Puah were Hebrews or Egyptians tending to Hebrew women's pregnancies. The one clue that many commentators use to justify calling them Hebrew is the fact that their names are Semitic. Given the length of time of the Hebrews' sojourn in Egypt and the nature of their oppression, the nurse midwives could very well be interracial, part Hebrew and part Egyptian. Such an interracial designation would account for the reason why Pharaoh thought that he could trust them to follow his command. It would also account for their determination to resist that command.

> The ambiguity of this phrase raises an ancient question: were they Hebrew or Egyptian? The names seem Semitic (and hence un-Egyptian); then, too, the use of "Hebrew" in the Bible usually occurs when a foreigner is talking about Israelites. Yet, the women's answer in v. 19 suggests that they are in fact Egyptians. Abravanel notes that Hebrew women would not be likely to kill Hebrew babies.[9]

"Shiprah and Puah not only stand out for their conscience but become the first to acknowledge the God in the book of Exodus. This is done before both Israel and Egypt do so."[10] This also points to the possibility that they were interracial— having some knowledge of the God of the Hebrews, even though they use another name. God's eventual blessing upon them affirms that this God is Yahweh.

With the reaction of Shiprah and Puah, the Pharaoh is unable to go forward with his plan, perhaps recognizing that he cannot count on the midwives for their loyalty either.

> Failing in his commissioning of special agents (midwives) to carry out his genocidal plan, Pharaoh finally must enlist "all his people" (v. 22), and shift the scene to a cosmic setting, the Nile. The stage is thus set for the birth, endangering and rescue of Moshe.[11]

Harper's Bible Commentary sees the story of the midwives as a way of segueing into the story of Moses, the main character of Exodus. It provides no additional commentary on the women themselves, only to note that the text refers to God as "the Lord" rather than as Yahweh, which may give a clue to the possibility that they are Egyptian rather than Israelites.[12]

The Women's Bible Commentary looks at the actions of Shiprah and Puah with a mixture of admiration and criticism aimed at the patriarchal structure and their place in it:

> Resistance to the Pharaoh's oppression of the Israelites begins with the refusal of the midwives Shiphrah and Puah to obey the royal order to kill all Hebrew boys at birth. . . . They are the only women in Exodus to act in an overtly political sphere, having direct contact with Pharaoh. . . . Such contact between the powerful ruler of an empire and two women who tend to the needs of slaves seems unlikely from a historical perspective. . . . As those who aid birth, they are the first to assist in the birth of the Israelite nation. Their work entails an understanding of the connection between transformation and risk, although the means by which they rebel against Pharaoh reiterates a biblical pattern of female deception.[13]

Traditional commentary as a rule identifies the actions of the women who refused to obey Pharaoh, but gives them no theological significance in terms of God' overall plan for deliverance of the Israelites.

Jochebed

"The woman conceived and bore a son; and when she saw that he was a fine baby, she hid him three months." (Exodus 2:2)

Very little is written about Jochebed even though she was the mother of one of the major characters in the Hebrew story. We know from Numbers 26:57–62 that she is descended from the house of Levi. She married Amram, her nephew. She was his father's sister (Ex. 6:20).

The Women's Bible Commentary includes Jochebed in the company of the other five women who saved Moses' life. Once again the major critique is that the names of these women, with the exception of the midwives, are not deemed important enough to be included in the initial narrative.

> Numerous women make their appearance in the Exodus narrative in conjunction with the childhood of Moses. It is these women who make possible the survival and growth of the central character in the Exodus narrative; yet, in contrast to Shiphrah and Puah, they are not named. They are presented as mother, sister, daughter, or servant. Here they are of interest only in their relationship to the male protagonist.[14]

Needless to say, without Jochebed there would be no story to tell about the baby Moses. It is her initial courage combined with the actions of the midwives, Miriam, and the Pharaoh's daughter that make the Moses narrative. Her determination to keep the baby is later rewarded, as she becomes a paid nursemaid for her own son. Traditional commentary writers overlook the poignant scene of the return of Moses to his birth mother by Pharaoh's daughter.

Miriam

"Then his sister said to Pharaoh's daughter, 'Shall I go and get you a nurse from the Hebrew women to nurse the child for you?' Pharaoh's daughter said to her, 'Yes.' So the girl went and called the child's mother." (Ex. 2:7–8)

Miriam is an intriguing presence in the Old Testament. She is the youthful sister who assists with the preparation of the basket for the infant Moses; she is the one who remains to find out who takes the baby in; she is the one who arranges for Moses' mother to nurse him into early childhood. She plays a pivotal role in the later story of Moses, as well. Following the deliverance into the promised land, she sings with joy and thanksgiving to Yahweh. Labeled as a prophetess, she challenges Moses about his prophetic exclusivity and chides him about his Cushite wife. Her role as one of the women who saves Moses' life is usually dwarfed by her later actions as prophetess, coliberator, and guardian of the Levite tradition.

Her role in Moses' early life and infancy is one that draws women into her corner as they proclaim her as one of the great women of the Bible. However, much of the commentary centers on her later actions—primarily the encounter with Moses in Numbers 12:1–15, in which she rebukes Moses for having a Cushite wife and threatens his position as the only one through whom God speaks.

Miriam brings forth two important issues about the Levite tradition, which she sees Moses as having broken. As a Levite, she attempts to stake her claim for becoming a member of the religious prophetic family. The other speaks to her conservative views about endogamy—marrying within the clan. Moses, obviously, has married a Cushite (Ethiopian). Many commentators have felt that this was not Zipporah, who was Midianite, but rather another wife. Rohl's controversial research gives some insight into the possibility of a Cushite wife for Moses.

If his research is accepted, then there is some reason to believe that before he was forty years old, Moses may have married a Cushite, prior to the deliverance story. Rohl's research places Moses in a leadership role in the Egyptian war with Ethiopia (Cush) during the 13th Dynasty of Kaneferree, Moses' stepfather. Such an expedition could have resulted in Moses taking an Ethiopian (or Cushite) wife.[15]

Other commentators have seen in the story of Miriam and her comments about the Cushite wife literary symbolism for the fate that Miriam will meet following this encounter.

At the same time, the relationship between the Cushite wife and Miriam, while oppositional on one level, also involves a transformational identification, signaled by the problematic disappearance of the strange wife after her brief mention in Numbers 12:1, coupled with the subsequent estrangement of the Israelite sister. Positing an identification between the Cushite wife and Miriam, the negativity associated with Miriam's punishment could be turned completely inside out and read as symbolic of rebirth.[16]

Other writers see this encounter between Moses and Miriam as a smokescreen camouflaging the real issue, which is who is entitled to be a vehicle for God's Word:

> The implicit question in this story is this: can prophetic or any other revelation override Mosaic revelation? In other words, is prophecy subordinate to the authority of Moses—the Mosaic tradition. . . . It is suggested that behind this story lies a conflict between specific priestly or prophetic groups in Israel's history.[17]

Miriam, then, plays a key role in the important debate regarding Mosaic versus prophetic voices in the wilderness.

The troubling aspect of this encounter is, however, the fact that Miriam receives the harshest treatment for her questioning of Moses. God punishes her by making her leprous for seven days, thus negating her prophetic call by making her ritually unclean. Conservatives who believe that women have no place in the priestly or pastoral role have used this scripture to justify their opposition to the ordination of women.

> Just as God makes an arbitrarily fine distinction not just between one tribe of Israelites (the Levites) and the others, but between lineages within that tribe (Aaron, not Korah), so also God picks and chooses within that lineage: Aaron, not Miriam. . . . Ascribed status—a

matter of birthright is by definition arbitrary; it is just as arbitrary as the punishment of Miriam and not Aaron, and is, in fact, modeled by the fates of those two characters. . . . The fact that Miriam is female is hardly irrelevant; however, Miriam's (female) impurity, her irrevocable difference, is simply made manifest, the reality of her strangeness to the patrilineage exposing the illusion of her insider blood.[18]

Later in Exodus we encounter Miriam again as she celebrates the Hebrews' freedom from Pharoah (Ex. 15:20–21). As Israel moves away from Egypt and closer to the promised land, she sings a song of deliverance—a song that is later attributed to Moses:

The Song of Miriam. Before the insertion of the entire Song of the Sea into the narrative, it was cited by its incipit in one of the prose sources . . . where it is ascribed to Miriam, the sister of Aaron and Moses. The attribution to Moses himself in v. 1a, therefore, is secondary.[19]

As is evident from this commentary, even Miriam's moment of celebration and song is overshadowed by Moses' receiving recognition for her Song of the Sea. Miriam is said to have died and her body buried in the wilderness of Zin in Kadesh (Num. 20:1), but not before acting as the catalyst to bring the two mothers of Moses together—the one who birthed him and the one who reared him, the one who had the courage to protect him from death and the one who had the courage to shield him from her own father. Miriam served as that vehicle through which God worked to bring about the deliverance of the Jews.

The Pharaoh's Daughter

"When the child grew up, she brought him to Pharaoh's daughter, and she took him as her son. She named him Moses, 'because,' she said, 'I drew him out of the water.'" (Ex. 2:10)

We know more about her father's work and punishment than we know about this daughter who was an integral part of the life of Moses. Having given him a life, Pharaoh's daughter made plans for his care, first by securing a nursemaid from among the Hebrews—Jochebed. Then she gave him a name after he was weaned.

> The name Moses from an Egyptian word meaning, "to beget a child" and perhaps once joined with the name of an Egyptian deity (compare the name Thut-Mose) is here (in the scripture) explained by the Hebrew verb meaning "to draw out." The narrator sees divine providence at work, causing the evil design of Pharaoh to serve God's purpose.[20]

While past commentators have not been able to name this Pharaoh's daughter, Rohl has once again discovered some new insight into the story. His research has found that Palmanothes, who was persecuting the Jews, had a daughter named Merris, who is known to have "adopted a Hebrew child who grew up to be called prince Mousos. Merris married a Pharaoh Khenephrês. Prince Mousos grew up to administer the land on behalf of this pharaoh. He led a military campaign against the Ethiopians who were invading Egypt; however, upon his return, Khenephrês grew jealous of his popularity. Mousos then fled to Arabia, to return when Khenephrês died and lead the Israelites to freedom."[21]

This is one of the few times when the possibility of the name of the Pharaoh's daughter has been mentioned by any commentator on the book of Exodus. Whatever her name, her courage and compassion speak to her strength and contribute to her intimate role in the fulfillment of God's plan for deliverance.

JUSTICE READING STRATEGY

The Moses event is one in which five women, through their disobedience and acts of resistance, affirmed life and provided hope. Through their efforts, God's will became manifest in the world. They became a pocket of resistance in the furtherance of God's plan for deliverance. Their liberation of Moses is a forerunner to the liberation of Israel. As a precursor to Moses' challenge to Pharaoh, they each in their own way also challenged him.

Mark William Olson writes this about the liberating Moses event:

> According to Exodus 1, Shiprah and Puah "feared God" and "did not do as the king of Egypt commanded them." Many centuries before Jesus, these brave women refused political intimidation. They "took up" the threats that political authorities used to try to control them, and walked in God's way. In so doing, they found joy. They fostered life. And they fomented hope. That's what taking up the cross is all about.[22]

It is easy to see how each of these women became a part of God's plan; however, another message is also inherent in the Moses event. It took women from different social, religious, racial, cultural, and class backgrounds to make this event happen. God's message here continues to resonate in our lives today as efforts for liberation increasingly must include intergenerational, interfaith, intercultural, interclass and interracial efforts to become a part of God's salvific plan for humanity.

IDA B. WELLS-BARNETT: SAYING "NO" TO LYNCHING

Ida Bell Wells-Barnett (1862–1931) was an advocate for human rights and women's suffrage. On both fronts she confronted a society that found her strong spirit and her bold actions problematic for the continued rule of white supremacy in American society. Ida B. Wells-Barnett was an unsung heroine of her time, but that never stopped her from seeking a change to what she saw as life-denying actions against African Americans.

Born in Holly Springs, Mississippi, Ida Bell Wells came of age in the Reconstruction and post-Reconstruction era. Educated and fiercely independent, Wells-Barnett used her talents as a journalist to champion the cause of civil rights and to fight the increasingly violent Jim Crow South, which had evolved in an effort to deny the African American population education and economic and political rights through intimidation and violence. In 1889, Wells-Barnett bought a one-third interest in a newspaper, the *Memphis Free Speech and Headlight,* and later became its editor.[23]

While on a trip out of town, three of her colleagues— grocery store owners—were lynched so that the white owner of a competing store could gain the business of the black community. The lynching started Wells-Barnett on a path that she would continue to pursue for most of her adult life—getting the United States to enact laws against lynching. However, prior to embarking on her crusade, Wells-Barnett was forbidden to return to Memphis after the death of her associates, because the white power structure in Memphis threatened to lynch her if she returned to publish her paper. Wells-Barnett remained in the North and later moved to Chicago, where she continued her activist and investigative journalistic efforts to outlaw lynching.

She, like most Americans, black and white, had believed that lynching happened to accused rapists—that is, black men accused of raping white women. Yet the men brutally murdered in Memphis had not been accused of rape. Instead, they were outstanding community citizens whose only crime was economic prosperity. Wells began to investigate cases in which lynch victims were accused of rape. She concluded that lynching was a racist device for eliminating financially independent black Americans.[24]

Wells-Barnett's attack on the American system of lynching was relentless and bare-bones honest. She cited numerous examples from her own experience as well as from southern newspapers. Meanwhile, white men seduced and raped black women without consequences. The same lynch mob that killed a Nashville black man accused of visiting a white woman left unharmed a white man convicted of raping an eight-year-old black girl. With scarcely suppressed rage, Wells-Barnett observed, "The outrage upon helpless childhood needed no avenging in the case, she was Black."[25]

Wells-Barnett did not stop her antilynching efforts, and she went on to become one of the founders of the National Association for the Advancement of Colored People (NAACP) in 1909. She was a founder of the Alpha Suffrage Club, an attempt to integrate the suffrage movement of Susan B. Anthony, which had aligned with southern white supremacist men in a pact to exclude black women from the franchise. She also founded the Chicago Settlement House, a precursor to the Chicago Urban League.

For her efforts, Ida B. Wells-Barnett was greeted with systemic threats of violence by the American white male power structure. She was one of the first to tie the violence against African Americans to their economic activities and advancements.

Banishment and demonization were the systemic tools used for those who attempted to suppress the works of Ida B. Wells-Barnett. She was looked upon as standing against the continued economic and legal oppression of blacks in the South and was thus feared by those in power. Her entrepreneurial efforts were thwarted momentarily when the white Memphis businessmen who had lynched her associates burned her newspaper business down. She was threatened with death should she return to Memphis, her home. The banishment came about because of her continued call for social justice and her refusal to be controlled by the threat of bodily harm.

The post-Reconstruction South was an economic disaster for white southerners, who were guarded by northern troops and handicapped by the loss of property and privilege. Even poor, southern whites had lost something—dignity. As blacks were elected and appointed to Congress and state legislatures, whites were struggling for survival. As the Freedman's Bureau built black schools and blacks took advantage of those opportunities, creating communities and building economic centers around segregated outlets, the desire of whites to regain economic prosperity grew faster than opportunities permitted. When the Hayes-Tilden compromise of the late 1800s took the federal troops out of the South, a reign of terror against blacks began. Sanctioned by a tacit governmental system that looked the other way, lynching and terror reigned throughout the South. The fear of the "other" took the form of murder and attempted genocide, especially toward black men. While many attributed it to racism, Ida B. Wells-Barnett's experience and her subsequent response of defiance gave it another face—economic envy on the part of whites.

The scholar René Girard calls this "the fundamental emotion of mimetic rivalry, envy inspired by a too-successful rival."[26] In this instance, the former slaves and especially the former enslaved women gained power, education, and access to a broader society that poor whites could not master nor enter because of lack of education and capital. The white southern response was terrorism. Even after the legal system acted on its behalf by removing troops from the South, eliminating the legislative and political advancements of blacks, the lynching continued.

The conditions that led to the vehement attack on Ida B. Wells-Barnett included the fact that the Jim Crow South was losing its grip on the economic and physical control over black men, but particularly black women. African American women had always been the unchallenged domain of white male oppressive structures. This was particularly true in the South. The slave owners took personal liberties with slave women, without penalty. This power was receding and, with that recession of power, the efforts of Ida B. Wells-Barnett required violent responses as the erosion of the southern white structure of Jim Crow was becoming endangered.

In this instance, the treatment of Wells-Barnett was nothing short of what was experienced by Vashti. The biblical text tells of her banishment and the Jewish Midrash tells of her death for her actions. While Wells-Barnett avoided Vashti's fate as described in the Midrash, she did experience that described in the Bible, but proceeded on with her resistance, not returning to the South until sometime during the twentieth century.

In her quest to save African Americans from lynching, Wells-Barnett confronted presidents, Congress, and members of state legislatures to enact antilynching laws. With the courage of the nurse midwives, she defied the power structure of the day in order to affirm the life of a people considered a threat by the powers of the day. She said "no" to the life-denying laws of the power structure.

THEOLOGICAL REFLECTION AND QUESTIONS

1. Many opponents of legalized abortions have used the stories of Shiprah and Puah to justify their attempts to break the laws permitting abortions. They have argued that, just like the nurse midwives, they are responding to an unjust law to obey God's higher law to preserve life. How would you respond to this argument?

2. What contemporary social situation would you equate to the story of Moses and infanticide, or other attempts to destroy males in a targeted ethnic group?

3. For many people, the issue of mixed race adoption is a concern. The concern centers around the perception that interracial adoptions might rob the child of contact with his/her cultural background. How do you view that argument in light of the Moses story and his ability or inability to rediscover his own heritage?

4. You have heard the saying "It takes a village to raise a child." How do you relate that to the intergenerational, interfaith, intercultural efforts that led to the protection of Moses? Discuss.

5. When you look at recent wars and the atrocities they engender, such as the murder of men and the rape of women, how do you compare that to the Pharaoh's edict to kill the boys but let the females live?

3

Michal

Losing Her Song in the Midst of the Resistance

SCRIPTURE READINGS
1 Samuel 14:49, 18:17–30, 19:8–17, 25:44
2 Samuel 3:13–16, 6:16–23
1 Chronicles 15:29

Michal is a woman who stood her ground and said "no" to her father so that God's choice of David as king would become manifest. But something happened to Michal between the time she said "no" to Saul and the time that David took her back from Paltiel, her second prearranged marriage. Michal lost her song. The David that she loved became the David that she "despised in her heart" upon her return. What was it that caused her feelings to take such a drastic turn? Could it be that the forced marriages that Saul orchestrated, first David, then Paltiel, turned a starry-eyed young girl into a bitter woman? Could it be that all of the politically arranged marriages that Saul used to control the life of Michal and boost his own grab to maintain power caused Michal to experience such bitterness and pain that she turned inwardly angry and distraught? Whatever the reason, what we know about Michal is that she once loved David and then she despised him in her heart.

Michal is an integral part of the story of the rise of David as King of Israel. Beginning with her introduction into the Hebrew Scriptures, the reader is made aware of Saul's attempts to use her as a tool to kill David. Once Saul has surmised that David is God's chosen, he creates schemes for killing him. However, much to the chagrin of Saul, both his son, Jonathan, and his daughter, Michal, love David enough to save him from their father's plans for murder.

This chapter looks at Michal, the first wife of David. Michal defied King Saul, her father, and saved David's life. Even though David was God's anointed, Michal was not rewarded for acts of resistance; rather, she was punished. First Saul married her off to another man, Paltiel, and later David cursed her, rendering her barren. Michal is indeed an enigmatic figure in the story of David.

RETELLING THE NARRATIVE

In 1 Samuel 18:17–30, Saul's plot to marry David off to one of his daughters is revealed. His first attempt is to offer him his oldest daughter, Merab. Saul thought that he could be certain of David's death if he sent him up against the Philistines. David, unaware of Saul's intent, felt undeserving but honored that Saul wanted him to be his son-in-law. However, Saul for some unknown reason gave Merab to another, Adriel, the Meholathite. Still preparing to entrap David, Saul saw that his daughter, Michal, loved David. This is said to have pleased Saul. He imagined that Michal's love would ensnare David. That Michal loved David is a rarity in arranged marriages. For a second time Saul offered to make David his son-in-law by way of marriage to Michal. The bride price for Michal would be one hundred Philistine foreskins. Once again David felt honored to be considered good enough to become the king's son-in-law. The scripture records that David was triumphant. He took his men and killed one hundred Philistines and brought back to Saul the bride price for Michal.

Saul gave Michal to David, but he became even more obsessed with his death because he knew that God was with David and that Michal loved him (1 Sam. 18:17–30). Angered, Saul intensified his vendetta. After that Saul tried to entice Jonathan into killing David but found out that Jonathan loved David, too. Then he tried to do it alone. Jonathan alerted David to Saul's plot. Jonathan attempted unsuccessfully to keep Saul from sinning by killing David. Although Saul agreed, he attempted again. David later narrowly escaped death by Saul, who tried to pierce him with a spear. He fled to Michal, who helped him escape through the window. Using an idol as a decoy, Michal placed a net of goat's hair on top of the doll and placed it in the bed. When Saul's messenger arrived to take David to be killed, Michal told them that David was sick. Saul became suspicious and discovered that Michal had deceived him.

Michal is not mentioned anymore in this book until the end, when in 1 Samuel 25:44 the scripture tells us that she is given in marriage to Palti (referred as Paltiel in 2 Samuel 3:15) son of Laish from Galim. Michal remained with Paltiel until after Saul's death, when the house of Saul, led in battle by Abner, surrendered to David. When David began to solidify his control over Israel after the death of Saul and a number of battles, Abner, the commander for the house of Saul, defected to David. Before accepting Saul's property and people, David demanded to have Michal delivered to him. David, however, had by this time six children by six other wives (2 Sam. 3:2–5). He also sent word to Saul's son Ishbaal, saying, "Give me my wife Michal to whom I was engaged at the price of one hundred foreskins of the Philistines" (2 Sam. 3:14).

Ishbaal took Michal from her husband Palti(el). When Abner went to get Michal, Paltiel followed behind them crying out for his wife, until Abner told him to go home. David continued to solidify his control over Israel. At his moment of triumph, when he is bringing the Ark of the Covenant into the city, as he dances and jumps with joy, Michal is at a window looking down on him, "despising him in her heart." (2 Sam. 6:16). Michal scolds David for his uninhibited display of dancing, naked, with the Ark. David corrects her and says it is before God that he is dancing and that he will continue to make a fool of himself before God. The text says that from that day on Michal was cursed by David and was rendered barren.

TRADITIONAL COMMENTARY

> Saul's immediate problem is the powerful intervention of his own children, first his son and then his daughter, who thwart him. In verses 2–7, Jonathan had been direct with Saul and persuasive in his rhetoric. Michal, by contrast, is devious and indirect, but equally effective.[1]

Even though biblical scholars have found it difficult to write about Michal without an overemphasis on David, they cannot help but be drawn to her pervasive presence and her personality throughout the beginning of the David narrative. Her presence starts at the very beginning of David's rise to power and shadows his conquest of Saul's kingdom. Michal is central to the transference of power from David to Saul. She is used by Saul to ensnare David and by David to legitimize his claim to Saul's kingdom. Always an object in the opinions of commentaries, Michal is seldom looked at as a possible subject in and of herself.

The scholar Walter Brueggemann is one of the exceptions to this observation. In Michal he sees a woman who takes initiative, where David fails to act.

Even in his desperate escape through a window, David takes no initiative to save himself. It is Michal who initiates the action; she lets him out the window so that he escapes from the guards posted by Saul. . . . Moreover, it is Michal who constructs the elaborate subterfuge to give David time to escape.[2]

The Women's Bible Commentary offers several excellent analyses of the role of Michal in the story of David. Besides seeing the relationship between David and Michal as a "puzzling one," the commentary talks about how Michal was used as a political and sexual pawn in the story of the transfer of power between David and Saul. Throughout the scripture, according to this commentary, depending upon the situation Michal is variously referred to as Saul's daughter and David's wife (even as she is being taken away from her second husband). Before David made his final bid for Israel, he asked for the return of Michal. The commentators try discerning exactly why David made such an effort:

> What are David's motives? The most obvious explanation for David's insistence on the return of Michal before he will enter into negotiations with Abner is that Michal was or could easily become a hostage. . . . If David still cared for Michal, he might have been afraid that Michal would become a victim of his overt attempt to capture the throne of Israel. It is also possible that Michal, as Saul's daughter, in some way legitimates David's claim to Saul's throne, so that it was not necessarily affection that prompted him to worry about her welfare before he accepted Abner's offer.[3]

The Women's Bible Commentary equates the actions taken against Michal by both her father and David as being a part of the overall political plan for gaining and maintaining control of Israel. Michal's response of contempt for David stems from this mix of "royal conflict and sexual conflict," according to Jo Ann Hackett, the author of the commentary. Michal is met with the specter of a scantily clad David rejoicing in the revelry of her father's kingdom, with her on display as a symbol of Saul's kingdom of old. Perhaps it is for this reason that she despises him in her heart. When she speaks, he curses her, meaning that she would be quiet from now on.[4]

The writer goes on to speculate about what David could have meant by the curse of barrenness—a curse that is usually made by God.

> It is not said whether Michal is unable to have children, an affliction generally believed to be from Yahweh, or whether David simply refuses to impregnate her. But whichever is meant, the punishment resembles the outburst in that it is for Michal both a sexual tragedy and a family tragedy, since it means that no children will be born to one of the few surviving offspring of Saul's house.[5]

Robert Cohn, the author of a commentary on 1 Samuel, sees in Michal independence as she protects David. It is the same independence that resurfaces as she admonishes him. "Michal here shows the independence that will later (2 Sam. 6) be turned against David."[6] Cohn then views Michal as a woman with some, if limited, personal power in the narrative.

David Gunn elaborates on the Michal theme in his commentary on 2 Samuel. He sees the encounter between David and Michal as a significant part of the chapter. Michal, who is referred to as "Saul's daughter" instead of "David's wife," recognizes her role as a part of the royal line of Saul. As she criticizes David for his display of himself in transporting the Ark of the Covenant through the city, we are reminded of her royalty. Gunn further sees David as acting hastily in his attempt to dismiss Michal's importance by cursing her with barrenness. In his comments, Gunn mentions that a son from

Michal would have legitimized David's rule over Israel upon his death. Instead David's sons end up battling over who should succeed him in his death. With a clear line to Saul, Gunn believes, such a battle would not have been necessary.[7]

The use of women as tools or pawns of war is one of the most demeaning experiences for women—yet it is one of the oldest. Saul in his attempt to kill David used his daughter Michal as bait to snare him. When Michal actually fell in love with David, Saul could no longer rely upon his scheme. Even though David escaped from the murderous clutches of Saul, he could not prevent Saul from using Michal again by giving her to one of his political allies. But David is not above using Michal either. His resolve to have her returned to him gives some indication that he could possibly be using her position as Saul's daughter to bring status to himself. It is not enough for him to have been anointed by God; David seems to need additional affirmation that he is king. In this respect his exchange with Michal and her reaction to him are understandable.

> The exchange between Michal and David is carefully crafted. She speaks sarcastically about "the king." . . . Michal speaks with authority, with an assumed voice of strength. Her speech concerns "honor" (glory), "the maids," and "uncovering shamelessly." Her words drip with sarcasm and anger. . . . Michal believes David has forfeited the respect he must have to be ruler. . . . David dismisses Michal and the entire Saulide claim.[8]

Michal's story is complicated. When we try to discern her role in the salvation story we stop after her attempt to save David's life. Her life after that is shrouded in power plays and kings seeking power. As we view the next section, it might be necessary to keep in mind that Michal had very little control over her own reality. Each time that she performed an act of resistance, she paid a price for it.

JUSTICE READING STRATEGY

Walter Brueggemann wrote about the story of David and Michal that it sounded like a soap opera, given all of the intrigue:

> We seem to be reading a dime store novel or watching a seedy soap opera. There is nothing here of God or God's will or God's coming Kingdom. We are treated to calculating human actions that do not conform to our expectations. Something is deeply awry when a future king must crawl through a window, when the wife of a coming king must lie to the father who is still king. The evil spirit of Saul has infected the whole scene.[9]

There can be some disagreement with this position held by Brueggemann; while Michal is a tragic figure, she is not a maudlin one. She is able to take control of her situation enough to save David's life and to protect her own dignity, even in the difficult place in which she found herself. Her initial actions are a part of God's will and of God's kingdom. Her deception is no greater than David's as we see his life unfold before us in scripture. Exhibiting loyalty to Saul after his use of her as a tool for gaining power is not a rational response, nor is exhibiting loyalty to David, given his use of her as a pawn in his grab for power over all of Israel.

In this section we will look at how Michal played a pivotal role in the unfolding of God's plan for humanity.

In the justice reading strategy it is clear that Michal is an instrument of God, rather than of two warring kings. Michal is an integral part of the salvation story. She stands both at the threshold and at the pinnacle of David's power. Her bold act of defiance makes way for God to continue unfolding the story of deliverance and salvation for Israel.

David, obviously, is not a perfect man or a perfect king, but that is not the point—he was chosen by God and is accountable to God for his actions. What Michal is able to do is to save David from one corrupt king and to be disapproving of his actions, which she sees as disrespectful to the kingship in which God placed him. With her courage to speak out about his actions, which matches her courage to hide him and save him from danger, Michal becomes a strong influence in the Bible. That both her father and her husband used her as a pawn is unfortunate for the portrayal of women in the Bible. On the other hand, she is no shrinking violet; she stands up for what she believes is morally right, and for that she fits well into the plan.

Attempts to reflect upon or analyze her according to her deception of Saul are meaningless, when we compare her to other biblical characters who have been similarly deceptive but have still served God in their actions—for example Rahab. Michal, though overlooked by many writers, proves to be a formidable candidate for one who is serving God's will in the biblical story of salvation and redemption.

WOMEN, RAPE, AND WAR

Michal was Saul's princess and David's queen, but her high standing in the Israelite tribe did not exempt her from being used as a bargaining chip for warring tribes. Whether it was Paltiel or David, she was a commodity to be used—as bait to entrap David and, in the case of Paltiel, perhaps as a way of solidifying a cooperative relationship with his father's tribe. While the word enslavement is not used to characterize her situation, it could be. She has lost the freedom to be in control of her own body and her own life. Most of us read the story as though it was only a historical accounting of another place and another time. Yet we can make comparisons to a world that has supposedly moved beyond such a practice, a more enlightened world.

Just as the Trokosi women of Ghana are considered slaves to the gods of the Ewe people, women in Pakistan also are enslaved by customs and tribal constraints. But before looking at the contemporary status of women as war objects, it is important to look at the history of another group of women who were sexual slaves for Japan's military. They were called "comfort women."

Former Comfort Women Say "No" to Japanese Coverup

Of course today, because of increased pressure by women, war time rape in the territory of the former Yugoslavia and in Rwanda is under serious scrutiny at the international tribunals established to address war crimes in those areas. And, as reported by the rapporteur, war rape in Kashmir by the Indian forces and in Burma by the [opposing force] is rampant. Even so, some governments have advanced the absurd notion that war-rape is a newly condemned crime. However, war rape in spite of its failure to have attracted sufficient remedial measures has been condemned in international law for centuries. The early scholars Belli (1563), Genmtili (1612) and Grotius (1625) all indicate that war rape was a war crime. The post World War I Versailles Commission listed rape as a war crime. Control Council Law No. 10, defining war crimes and listing crimes against humanity for the Nuremberg and Tokyo Charters, includes war rape.[10]

Attorney Karen Parker was speaking in this passage before the United Nations as an advocate for the rights of the women known as "comfort women" during World War II. She was petitioning Japan for compensation to the surviving victims and the families of those women upon whom war crimes of rape were committed. During the Second World War, the Japanese army established its own brothels for the military men. Nearly eighty thousand to two hundred thousand "comfort women" were lured to military bases, thinking that they were going to get jobs in a factory. Over 75 percent of the women were Koreans; the rest were a combination of Japanese, Taiwanese, Filipinos, Indonesians, Dutch, Burmese, and Pacific Islanders. In 1948 a tribunal was held to examine the issues surrounding the comfort women. The case was brought on behalf of seventy-five Dutch women, no others. The result was that a few Japanese military officers were convicted of war crimes against these seventy-five women. However, the plight of the remainder of the women was not included in that tribunal. As late as 1990, the governments of Japan and Korea denied ever having the camps.[11]

From Parker's recitation of the statistics and the history of the comfort women, it is amazing that any are left to tell the story. "A minimum of 125 million rapes [occurred]—maybe even twice that many. . . . At an average of ten rapes per day (still a low figure) in a five-day work week, each comfort girl was raped fifty times per week or 2,500 times per year. For three years of service—the average—a comfort girl was raped 7,500 times."[12]

In the late 1980s the former comfort women said "no" to the silence surrounding their plight. They organized and gained worldwide publicity around their issue. They petitioned the Japanese government with demands that included: an end to the cover-up; a public apology; complete disclosure of what happened; a memorial to the victims; compensation for survivors or families; a rewriting of Japanese history to include the story of the comfort women; and a commitment that such brutality would never occur again.

The Japanese government has yet to fully disclose the horrors of the comfort women's plight during the war. Consequently, the women's struggle continues and their resilence and demand for justice grow more each day. With the global community looking on, these women continue to foment acts of everyday resistance against the Japanese government in hopes that their demands will be met.

Pakistan and the Bartering of Young Girls

The Khans are a group of Pakistanis in the Abba Keel villages who have separated themselves into two warring camps—the

Hussain Khans and the Noor Khans. The *Newsweek* article that reported on the Khans described the beginning of this feud in this way:

> One of the Khan brothers Atta was sentenced to life in prison, and an uneasy truce prevailed for the next 30 years. Then a property dispute stirred up old grudges. Atta was out of jail on parole by then, and Bahadur's brother Sardar—Wazira's father—decided to settle old scores. He and three cousins laid an ambush for Atta. They missed and killed Atta's brother and one of his nephews instead. Sardar and his accomplices were caught, tried and sentenced to die.
>
> Under Pakistani law, convicted murderers can bargain with the victims' families for a reprieve. The Noors demanded 8 million rupes (about $130,000) and eight of the condemned men's daughters in marriage. Tasneem and Wazira, the first girl in her family ever to finish high school, were the oldest. The others ranged from 2 to 9. Their weddings were held, too, but by local custom the consummation was postponed until puberty. . . . The girls were included just to inflict humiliation on them.[13]

It is always difficult for Western women to understand arranged marriages, and certainly they can not fathom being traded for the benefit of adversarial relationships between tribes and clans of people. However, in a large part of the developing world and many areas in more developed countries, people speak of such marital arrangements.

In the twentieth and the beginning of the twenty-first centuries, the world is reminded of the plight of women and girls during war time. Bosnia, Rwanda, and Croatia all provided the world with a look at what happens to women in the middle of wars of ethnic cleansing—they are raped, taken away from their families, and bear children who are mixed race as a way of compromising one group with a new generation of children with a lack of cultural identity.

War not only brings out the worst in those fighting the battles, it also spreads that spirit of "conquer or be conquered" to the wombs of women—through rape, forced marriage, and the removal of any semblance of self-respect. If Michal had this kind of thinking in the back of her mind, one can see how she managed to look at David and despise him in her heart.

CONCLUSION

This chapter has attempted to look at the story of Michal and her role in salvation history. It is important to note that Michal once had the freedom to love. So in love was she that she deceived and disobeyed her father in order to keep David alive. As we find out later, David retrieves her as though she were a lost piece of property. She is recovered and when she expresses an opinion she is cursed by David and rendered barren. The final consequences notwithstanding, Michal contributes to God's plan for salvation, losing in the process her song—her joy.

Michal was a tool of war, not unlike the women of the Noor tribe of Pakistan, the comfort women of Japan, and the women and girls of the Croatian, Rwandan, and Serbian wars of the twentieth and twenty-first centuries. They are our contemporaries and they are still living at a time when women have no control of their bodies or their lives. Everyday small acts of resistance, it would seem, are necessary to keep their spirits alive and to fulfill God's call for justice.

THEOLOGICAL REFLECTION AND QUESTIONS

1. How would you describe Michal's movement from "loving" David to "despising him in her heart?" What could have caused such a drastic shift in affection? How do you personally relate to such a drastic turn in a relationship? Have you ever experienced such a dynamic?

2. Through all her trials and tribulations, Michal actually lost her "song," or some might say she lost her "joy." Are there times when you believe that you have lost your song or your joy? If so, when and why?

3. If you were using this scripture as a part of a counseling session for newlyweds, how would you use the story of Michal and David to give them warnings about some of the pitfalls in marriage?

4. Michal disobeyed her father in order to save David's life. How would you characterize her role in God's salvation story?

5. Michal was a woman who had very little control over her life. Her father gave her to David in marriage for his own political aims and then, while David was exiled, he gave her to Paltiel. Can you envision the range of her emotions about her own personal freedom? Explain.

4

The Daughters of Zelophehad

Women Who Say "No" to Economic Injustice

SCRIPTURE READINGS
Numbers 26:33, 27:1–11, 36:1–11
Joshua 17:1–6
1 Chronicles 7:15

54

"As unmarried women whose father has died, they have little or no power or standing in the Israelite community. Perhaps they show the boldness of those who have nothing to lose."[1]

The status of women in Hebrew society depended in large measure on their fathers and their husbands. They were accepted and acceptable as participants in the economic life of the family as long as they were connected in some way to either a husband or father. The five daughters of Zelophehad had neither. Their father had died in the wilderness awaiting the promised land while the daughters were still unmarried. Zelophehad was a descendant of Manasseh. (1 Chron. 7:15)

The mere fact that Moses and Eleazar the priest were at a loss as to how to respond to the five daughters speaks to the entrenched patriarchal society that was about to be formed in the new land. The women, whose names were Mahlah, Noah, Hoglah, Milcah, and Tirzah were descendants of Joseph and his Egyptian wife Asenath. Members of the clan of Manasseh, they were a part of the mixed culture of Egypt and Israel.

The story unfolds during the crucial period in the wilderness as the planning begins for the movement into Canaan. God has told Moses that he will not make it to the promised land and that the new generation will be its inhabitants. Mahlah, Noah, Hoglah, Milcah, and Tirzah are a part of that new generation and Moses' decision with God's help sets the stage for some of the changes that will take place within that new society. After consulting Yahweh, Moses gives the land allotted to the tribe of Manasseh to the five female heirs. We discover later on in the scriptures that no matter how rewarding the turn of events might seem, there were still restrictions placed on the daughters of Zelophehad—they had to marry within the clan, establishing endogamy (marriage within the clan) within the promised land culture. This final restriction was in keeping with Yahweh's intention for the land—that each clan would maintain a clear line of ownership.

Once in the promised land, the daughters had to remind Joshua, Eleazer the priest, and the leaders that they were, indeed, the rightful heirs. In Joshua 17, we find the five sisters speaking with authority:

"They came before the priest Eleazar, Joshua son of Nun and the leaders, and said, 'The Lord commanded Moses to give us an inheritance along with our male kin.' So according to the commandment of the Lord he gave them an inheritance among the kinsmen of their father." (Josh. 17:4). The daughters of Zelophehad took control of the land that extended from Asher to Micmethath east of Shechem. (Josh. 17:7).

About their victory, one commentator responds in this way:

> From the narrator's viewpoint, the daughters of Zelophehad, obedient to God, lived happy ever after, this calls for careful theological reflection. The daughters of Zelophehad and other women like them were granted a fresh option through land holding; yet restrictions were imposed.[2]

This chapter discusses the story of the petition made to Moses and Eleazar the priest by Zelophehad's daughters. When confronted with the petition to give Zelophehad's land to his daughters, in the absence of male heirs, a baffled Moses consulted with Yahweh on such an extraordinary issue. Yahweh commanded him to go forth and give the land to the daughters. Yahweh's response changed the dynamic of the economic status of women in the new generation. Following the justice reading strategy, we look at a contemporary issue of economic injustice in Nigeria.

RETELLING THE NARRATIVE

Their names were Mahlah, which means gentleness; Noah, which means flattery; Hoglah, which means magpie; Milcah, which means counsel; and Tirzah, which means delight.[3] They were born to the clan of Manasseh, descendants of Joseph and Asenath, his Egyptian wife. Asenath, whose name means "she belongs to (the goddess) Neith," was from On—a city ten miles northeast of present-day Cairo.[4]

These daughters, then, were women of color—part Israelite, part Egyptian. As Moses was dividing the promised land among the twelve tribes, he parceled out the land to the sons of this new generation, because according to custom and law, the land was to be transferred through the male heirs only.

Zelophehad, however, had daughters, not sons. At the time that they approached Moses, the five sisters were the only potential heirs of the clan of Manasseh. They asked Moses and Eleazar the priest why it was that they could not have land since their father had no sons. Moses, not knowing how to respond, went to Yahweh and asked what should he do. Yahweh told Moses that the daughters were right; they should receive the land, if there were no sons. With this strong affirmation from God, Moses parceled out the land to the daughters of Zelophehad.

The last chapter in Numbers revisits the issue of the daughters of Zelophehad and their inherited land. At that time Moses imposes one restriction on their inheritance of the land—they must marry within the tribe of Manasseh. So even though they had control of the land, they were not free to marry whom they pleased. Marriage for them would have to be within their own clan in order to maintain control of their land. The request of the daughters opened up a whole new economic opportunity for women in the future Israel, for it allowed them to actually take control of inherited property. The scripture tells us that later they married the sons of their father's brother in accordance with the restrictions placed on them. The daughters are mentioned again once in Canaan. This time they speak for themselves, as they remind Joshua of Moses' promise and pledge of the land while in the wilderness.

TRADITIONAL COMMENTARY

The censuses function to show that the size of the Israelite community remained constant through the wilderness period. The basis for land distribution in the land of promise will be the ancestral houses identified in the second census. In this context women and their concerns play a key role, as the daughters of Zelophehad ask whether women may receive land if there are no male heirs.[5]

Katharine Sakenfeld, a Princeton Theological Seminary Old Testament scholar, makes the point that the five Zelophehad sisters play a pivotal role representing the interests and concerns of women in the distribution of land. As a part of the second census of the wilderness population, the women are unique in their victory according to Danna Nolan Fewell, who writes in *The Women's Bible Commentary:* "Land ownership and inheritance are also rights belonging to men, passing patrilineally from generation to generation. Achsah and the daughters of Zelophehad are exceptions to the rule."[6] Fewell continues to dwell on the marginality of biblical women, rather than see hope in the bold actions of the five sisters.

Old Testament scholar Dennis Olson lists three themes in the daughters of Zelophehad scriptures: "(1) a reaffirmation of God's promise of the land; (2) a concern for the inclusiveness of all the tribes; and (3) a model of critical and creative affirmation of tradition."[7]

Olson is unique among commentary writers, however, because he actually focuses on the actions of the daughters and the courage that it took for them to speak up for themselves in their encounter with the great liberator, Moses.

> The five bold women who bring their case before Moses in Numbers 22 provide a model for the new generation. . . . these women are models of boldness fueled by hope, models of advocacy fueled by a concern for the larger community, and models of faithfulness fueled by a dynamic relationship with their tradition and with their God.[8]

Olson's sensitivity to the larger issue of women's economic status in the emerging promised land society is rare among scholars who comment on the book of Numbers. Most other commentaries on the daughters of Zelophehad are generally a subtext to the overall critique and analyses of the wilderness experience. Scholars other than feminist and womanist writers

are primarily concerned with the overall story of the establish-
ment of law and customs within the promised land—generally
focusing on the task set before Moses during his final days in
the wilderness.

> Most of chapters 26–36 have to do with instructions
> for how to live in the land of the promise: The army
> that is to take the land (Ch. 26), rules of inheritance
> of the land (27:1–11, Ch. 36); a festival calendar for
> the land (Ch. 32; 34), Levitical cities and cities of
> sanctuary in the land (Ch. 35)."[9]

Harper's Bible Commentary digs a little deeper and looks at
the dilemma faced by Moses. The writer's view the situation as
one in which Moses is making a choice between two distinct
inheritance laws—the laws of patrilineal inheritance versus
clan entitlement.

> Faced with this dilemma, Moses consults God for in-
> struction on this unprecedented case. Is it more im-
> portant that only males inherit property or that the
> land remain in the same family? God agrees with the
> daughters that the land must remain in their family's
> possession, even if it means violating the other custom
> that only males receive inherited land (27:5–11).[10]

In this commentary the writer minimizes the importance
of the daughters' request and emphasizes instead the decision-
making of Moses as he encounters these two points of view.
Not even their courage in confronting the daunting Moses
and the priest Eleazar give the commentators a different perspective from which to analyze the text. Filtering analysis and
exegesis through a patriarchal lens has been the major criticism
of this type of commentary. In such instances, the emphasis is
placed on Moses rather than the characters surrounding
him—in this case the daughters of Zelophehad. To compen-
sate for such commentary, feminist and womanist writers have

gone to the other extreme. Much of their writing has criticized the patriarchal approach without really attaching significance to the women, their actions, and their role in God's plan for redemption. The following is typical of such critiques:

> The women themselves are pictured as taking action for the sake of their father's name, not for the sake of their own opportunity to possess land. This story could be heard even in ancient Israel as a story of comfort for women who would not be left destitute but it was preserved primarily as a story of comfort for men who had the misfortune not to bear male heirs—their names would not be cut off from their clans.[11]

For a more comprehensive approach to the narrative, a return to Olson's commentary is in order. He writes:

> Two competing customs in laws are at work in this dispute. One custom in ancient Israel in its patrilineal system was that only males could inherit property. On the other hand, there is the high priority of keeping land with the original clans and tribes . . . determination is beyond human competence, the decision is left in the hands of God.[12]

In each instance mentioned, the story of the daughters of Zelophehad is analyzed according to the hermeneutic of a particular theological space. While it is legitimate for commentators to exercise their own theological perspective, it still does not provide a holistic look at the unique story and role played by Milcah, Mahlah, Noah, Hoglah, and Tirzah in God's plan for salvation.

THE JUSTICE READING STRATEGY

The justice reading strategy goes a bit further than the other commentaries. When looking at the scripture through this lens, it becomes clear that the daughters of Zelophehad decided to say "no" to economic injustice. Gender should not have been an issue to ensure parity among the tribes. God was clear and emphatic about the role of women in the distribution of the promised land when he commanded Moses to grant the land to the daughters. The women, feeling the power of God on their side, were able to reaffirm God's intention for the land once the Israelites crossed over to Canaan.

In acknowledging God's response, the daughters of Zelophehad were clearly changing the nature of the future for women in the Israelite community. The promised land would not only be populated by a new generation of the wilderness people, but it would also bring new understandings about the relationship between men and women and their place in God's unfolding plan for liberation and salvation. Salvation would not be for men alone. Women would actually receive a part of the land that God had promised. Through the daughters of Zelophehad, God spoke an affirming word about the inheritance of all of God's people in the making of the new home of the Israelites.

Their "no" to Moses' original plan meant that doors would open for women that had not been opened before. While there is no evidence that other women in similar situations received land, they nevertheless had the precedence of Milcah, Tirzah, Noah, Mahlah, and Hoglah to rely upon. They would now share in the covenant. There is no sense that God hesitated in responding to Moses. In other words, God's plan for all of God's creation was affirmed through this action. The women were used as a catalyst to redefine and reshape the Israelite society based on the equality of men and women to own land.

Once again, working through the least likely, the marginalized women, God gives a glimpse of a world where gender parity is the desired state for humanity. In spite of the final chapter of Numbers in which the daughters find themselves restricted in marriage—a cultural practice that is not altered or adjusted—the new economic order is in line with the new direction of the people of Israel. The new generation is ushered in through the removal of barriers to inheritance for women. God uses the five women to give Israel a glimpse of a reality that heretofore had escaped them. Milcah, Mahlah, Noah, Hoglah, and Tirzah are the vessels that God used to speak to a new generation about the need to share in God's riches with all of God's creation.

NIGERIAN WOMEN SAY "NO" TO ECONOMIC INJUSTICE

Escavos, or Ogborodo, is located in Warri, Nigeria. Nigeria is one of the world's top ten oil producers. Yet the economic conditions in villages in which transnational oil producers such as Chevron and Shell drill and transport oil has been polluted and the livelihood of the people destroyed.

Inhabitants of the Escravos community are mainly the Itsekiri, Ijaw, Yoruba, and Ilajes. Their occupation is fishing; consequently, the oil spills from the companies have a direct impact on the livelihood of the villagers. Most of the women are independent fish merchants, as well as mothers and wives. The oil spills affect their quality of life and those of their children. Economically, physically, and environmentally, the companies polluted the streams, the air, and the land, making it unbearable for adults and children to live without threats to their health and their quality of life. In addition, the women complained that the multimillion dollar company employed very few of the local people in the plant and disregarded the welfare of the village.

> We live by the grace of God. We used to sell fish at Escravos. We used to supply fish to people. Because of the oil spill in the area, we travel through boat for 150 kilometres into the sea before we can get fish. But after the crisis we've not done anything, we're stranded doing nothing. All of our money was burnt down. All

we have now are our children and husbands, we don't have any capital to start any business. Before Chevron came we had plenty of fish. But due to spillage fish had become scarce. The spillage has sunk into the soil so that it has become infertile and nothing can grow in the soil again. (Mrs. Esther Esimajete, a fisherwoman at Escravos as recorded in a hearing before the Environmental Rights Action)[13]

What Chevron is doing to us is wrong. The pollution from Chevron makes our children sick. They also inhale horrible fumes from the gas flares coming from Chevron's installations. Because of these, children have liver problems, bad eyesight, itching, and patchy complexion. The air of Ugborodo is very corrosive yet they've refused to pay us the money of the land they bought from us. No compensation has been paid the women. (Mrs. Oluch, secretary, Escravos women wing)[14]

It is well documented and well known that economic parity between women and men is nonexistent, even in the West. The diminished quality of life caused by economic injustice, however, is generally more prevalent in developing countries than in the West. In many of these countries, it is not only their own government that keeps women below men in wages or opportunities; but tribal customs, family structures, and globalization contribute to and exacerbate the inequality.

In the summer of 2002, one group of women said "no" to continued economic exploitation and injustice by multinational oil conglomerates Chevron/Texaco and Shell. These women refused to rest until they received an answer. It began in Ugborodo (Escravos), Nigeria, in the oil-rich Niger Delta when over a hundred women threatened to take off their clothes and go naked as a part of their nonviolent protest against the oil conglomerates. During the course of one week the all-women protest had staged nonviolent sit-ins at a half-dozen oil plants in the region. The first demonstration lasted ten days, as an intergenerational (the oldest in her nineties) group of women blocked the entrance to Chevron/Texaco's facilities and refused to leave.

It was a story that played around the world, giving courage and spiritual sustenance to other women who had been oppressed in much the same way. The women were able to get an audience with the senior executives of Chevron to negotiate with them about their demands, which included employment for village residents, investment in electricity for the village, assistance in reestablishing poultry and fish farms, and other infrastructure development. The women were the latest in a stream of protest that had taken place over the years. Most protests were carried out by men and involved violence and intimidation. The men had tried other tactics to get the multinational oil companies to bridge the gap between the nearly seventy-billion-dollar-a-year industry and the destitute poverty of the villages in which the plants occupy space and drill oil. The industry shared a portion of its profits with the government, but nothing filtered down to the people. As a matter of fact, the protests of the men resulted in the government protecting the industry and sentencing many of the protestors to death or imprisonment. The women were wise enough to employ nonviolent means for their protests.

The women achieved a modicum of success as a result of their nonviolent protest, but like the daughters of Zelophehad, they still had constraints that would keep them from achieving a full measure of justice. Their struggle for economic justice continues.

CONCLUSION

Whether it is the daughters of Zelophehad or the women of Nigeria saying "no" to economic injustice, women must continue acts of resistance when their God-given promise of an abundant life is threatened or taken away. It is a part of their role in the fulfillment of God's plan for all of God's created humanity. The message in the scripture from the daughters of Zelophehad speaks not only to their request of Moses, but of their bold action to become a part of a new generation of women who would have equal footing in the land promised to Israel. They, too, were a part of the covenantal community. They, too, were a part of the new generation coming out of the wilderness. They, too, were in God's unfolding plan.

As the spotlight is turned on women in developing countries, their model, their paradigm, speaks to women globally. Women who have been saying "yes" to economic injustice can look at the women of Nigeria and change their own economic exploitation. Just as the daughters of Zelophehad stood up to Moses, Eleazer, and Joshua, other women today can gain the courage to usher in a new economic order in their patriarchal cultures. They can look up from the Bible and see the contemporary resistance of the Nigerian women and envision for themselves and their children new economic possibilities. The contemporary action of the Nigerian women of Escravos in the oil-rich Niger Delta proves to be an inspiration for all women who seek economic justice. While their struggle might be a long one, they embarked upon it with the determination to change their lives and those of their children. Certainly, these women deserve to be a part of the long list of daughters of resistance.

THEOLOGICAL REFLECTION AND QUESTIONS

1. In many countries, the inheritance of property is still left in the hands of men alone. What has been your experience with property and the economic control of it by women?

2. Economic justice is elusive for many women, particularly women of color and third world women—what is your response to the presence of economic injustice in the world for these women?

3. How would you use God's affirmation of the economic quest of the daughters of Zelophehad to further the cause of economic justice for women?

4. How were the daughters of Zelophehad used in the furtherance of God's salvific plan for humankind?

5. Moses was baffled by the request of the daughters of Zelophehad. Why? How would you use this story in a Bible study for women with a background of low self-esteem and economic deprivation?

5

Susanna

God Rewards the Faithful

SCRIPTURE READINGS
Susanna, the Apocryphal/Deuterocanonical Books

The book of Susanna is found in the Apocryphal **67** writings and is subtitled and sometimes referred to as the thirteenth chapter of the book of Daniel. Daniel, the only apocalyptic writing in the Hebrew Scriptures, contains stories of hope for Jews during the Babylonian exile. The narratives highlight the rewards bestowed by God upon the faithful. The story of Susanna is one such narrative. The Apocryphal writings were penned during the period between 250 B.C.E. and 200 C.E. by Greek-speaking Jews, most of whom lived in Egypt. There is little to no evidence to support the possibility that Susanna was written initially in Hebrew. The Apocrypha, meaning "hidden" in Greek, refers to thirteen to fifteen books that were included in the Greek translations of the Hebrew Bible—two of which are the Septuagint (LXX) and the Theodotion. The LXX includes two sections, the Hebrew Bible translated into Greek and the additions made to the Hebrew Bible in the form of the Apocryphal writings. The LXX was, up until the second century, the only Greek translation of the Old Testament. In the years that followed, other Greek translations were written—one was called the Theodotion, which was translated toward the end of the second century. These Greek translations served the Jews of the diaspora who had, in many instances, lost their ability to read Hebrew. The Theodotion varies in some of its narrative content from the LXX but contains the same subject matter.[1]

Most English versions of the Susanna scripture are taken from the Theodotion translation. This chapter will discuss the story as it appears in the New Revised Standard Version of the Bible that uses the Theodotion translation. However, it is important to note a few of the distinctions that exist between the Theodotion and the LXX versions. The differences in the two texts center around the location of the trial (the LXX places the trial in the synagogue, while the Theodotion places it in the home of Joakim, Susanna's husband); the naming of Susanna (the LXX refers to her as the Jewess but the Theodotion names Susanna throughout the narrative, giving her a more personal identity); the age distinction between Daniel and the elders, which is more pronounced in the LXX, making the reader more aware of the innocence of Daniel and the corruption of the elders; and the contrast between the faithfulness of Susanna and the sins of the elders—more of a theme in the LXX than in the Theodotion. The final significant distinction is in the placement of the Book of Susanna. The story of Susanna is found after Daniel 12 in the LXX, before Daniel 1 in the Theodotion.

Susanna is a story of stark theological and ethical contrasts—youth versus the elderly as God's vehicle for the dispensing of wisdom; truth versus untruth; justice versus injustice; spiritual power versus institutional power; corruption versus righteousness; and the fear of humanity versus the fear of God. Many of these themes find their way into the commentaries on the book of Susanna.

RETELLING THE NARRATIVE

The setting for Susanna is Babylon during the Jewish exile at a date that is nonspecific. As in the other books of Daniel, the story is an attempt to lift the spirits of the faithful during this time of trial and dispersion through stories of hope and deliverance. The story is about a beautiful woman named Susanna (lily) who is married to Joakim (the Lord will establish), a prominent and prosperous Jew. Even in the midst of exile, many Jews flourished financially. Joakim was one of them. The writer takes pains to tell us that Susanna was taught the laws of Moses and feared God. This claim becomes critical as the story unfolds.

The stage is also set for the elders by the scriptures' characterization of them: "Wickedness came forth from Babylon, from elders who were judges, who were supposed to govern the people" (v. 5). In the home of Joakim and Susanna, the elders were frequently in and out trying cases for the people. Susanna would wait for the people to leave at noon, at which time she would go to her garden and bathe. The elders would watch her going to and fro and would each individually lust for her.

The scripture says "they suppressed their consciences and turned away their eyes from looking to Heaven or remembering their duty to administer justice" (v. 9).

One day as Susanna was bathing, the judges approached her to ask her to lay with them. They threatened that if she did not lay with them, they would falsely accuse her of adultery. Because Susanna feared God more than she feared the elders, she told them that she would rather disobey them, no matter what the consequences, than to disobey God. At this point, she cried out loud and the elders shouted against her. The people came out to see what had happened. The elders lied and told their story of Susanna's alleged adultery. According to Mosaic law, adultery was an offense punishable by death. (Deut. 22:22). When they told the people that Susanna had been caught under a tree with a young man, the elders knew that they were sentencing her to death.

The following day, the elders sent for Susanna to come before the people. She came with her children, her parents, and all her relatives, properly veiled. The elders demanded that she remove the veil; when she did, they gazed on her beauty once again as they began to give false testimony against her. Because they were the elders, the people believed them and condemned her to death (v. 41).

> Upon hearing the sentence, Susanna "cried out with a loud voice, and said, 'O eternal God, you know what is secret and are aware of all things before they come to be; you know that these men have given false evidence against me. And now I am to die, though I have done none of the wicked things that they have charged against me!' The Lord heard her cry." (vv. 42–44).

God, working through the Holy Spirit, reached Daniel. As they were planning to execute her, Daniel, overcome by the Holy Spirit, appeared and stopped the judges from going on with the execution. Daniel proclaimed that Susanna had not had a fair trial, according to the law of Moses. Acting as judge, Daniel convened a trial.

During the trial Daniel questioned the elders, prefacing his remarks by accusing them of past corruption. Daniel asked each judge, separately, what kind of tree was Susanna under with the young man? They each gave a different answer. With that indictment of themselves, Daniel sentenced them both to death. Susanna was vindicated and her faith in God was rewarded by her acquittal. Both judges were executed in Susanna's stead. The story proclaims the wisdom of Daniel in seeking a trial in order to exact justice; as such, it has traditionally been a story about his wisdom.

TRADITIONAL COMMENTARY

Contemporary readers of the Bible may very well overlook the Book of Susanna, but there was a time when it gave inspiration to Renaissance artists, poets, and theologians. It resulted in the outpouring of Renaissance paintings, literature, and poetic renditions of the scripture. While the secular world found intrigue in the story and took artistic license in its many versions, much of the religious commentary focused on the exploits of Daniel—his wisdom, justice, and call from God in his youth. Theological commentary also tends to be consistent with the story line of Daniel's other narratives—hope for the faithful Jews of the diaspora and proof that God invested wisdom in Daniel to deliver the faithful from death and danger. Susanna added an additional dimension to the Daniel message—that of the youthful Daniel emboldened by the gift of wisdom and the Holy Spirit even at a young age.

> While innocence and vulnerability may be generic to youth itself, it is God (Theodotion) or an angel (Septuagint)—who inspires youth with a spirit of insight and understanding, integrity and courage.[2]

Daniel's wisdom is usually contrasted with that of the elders and his youth is compared to their age. His move to exact justice makes a mockery of the role of the elders as judges over the people. That God has transferred the wisdom to the young in lieu of the old reflects upon the changing times during the exile and engenders hope in the future of the people of the diaspora.

> Daniel shows considerable acumen in refusing to accept the surface appearances at the trial, and he is clever in determining a way to get at the truth. We today might make the point by saying that Daniel is very smart. But smart is not the same as wise, and acu-

men and cleverness are insufficient for wisdom. Even a corrupt but clever lawyer might do what Daniel did; special moral discernment is not needed here . . . special moral discernment is needed and is shown in Susanna's case, however.[3]

While the theological reflection on the Book of Susanna has centered on Daniel, whose name means God is judge, her story has enchanted artists, poets, songwriters, and literary aficionados for many years.

The general popularity of this tale in Christian culture suggests not only its inherent attractiveness, but also certain plasticity: its elements can be shaped to serve different religious, social, and aesthetic ends. . . . Accounts of Susanna appeared in a variety of forms in Renaissance England: popular wall pictures, ballads, and drama.[4]

Some scholars have even suggested that the attention paid to Susanna by artists borders on the obsession of the elders. "It took a Connecticut Yankee poet, both inventive and alert to moments of individual crisis, to demonstrate how Americans have long resisted peering at Susanna in ways that replicate the elders leering gaze, and to suggest why he and others would instead join their voices with hers, singing Hosanna in her praise."[5]

The symbolism of Susanna has also provoked interpretations that are beyond the ordinary for biblical literature. For example, the Leviticus codes tell us that when a woman is being sexually attacked, she should cry out in a loud voice. This response assures all within earshot that she is being forced against her will. For Susanna, we hear two cries—the first when the elders approach her to seduce her and the second when she cries aloud to God and Daniel is sent through the Holy Spirit to respond. For Susanna the loud cry is the last that we hear from her. Daniel's follows her loud cry—"he shouted with a loud voice, 'I want no part in shedding this woman's blood'" (v. 46).

Crucially, Susanna does not offer a single version to counter the elders. Her response is the very act of raising "a loud voice"—a phrase that is used four times in this story (24; 42; 46; 60). It is her powerful voice personally raised in one terrible crisis, that Susanna insists that the possibility of particular versions—hers and others'—remain open. A most striking feature of Susanna and the elders is, indeed, the way that Susanna in her crucial garden scene and again in her public trial establishes the terms for all that follows. Her own example is reenacted in the language used when Daniel comes to judgment. When Daniel speaks before the town, he does so, we are told, "with a loud voice."[6]

The feminist commentary is predictable in that it centers on the patriarchy of the culture and power of the elders. For many feminists, the battle between Susanna and the elders reaffirms the powerlessness of biblical women. Many point to the scripture and believe that it is not only a story about lust and false witnessing, but one about the inability of a woman to extricate herself from the power of men in authority. In an article entitled "Sexuality and Social Control: Anthropological Reflections on the Book of Susanna," Susan Sered and Samuel Cooper view the narrative through the lens of gender politics:

> The story of Susanna is fundamentally a gendered story. The gender identities of the protagonist (Susanna), her champion (Daniel) and the villains (the Elders) are crucial to the cultural message, which the story conveys. The particular danger which threatens Susanna is a gendered danger (rape). . . . Susanna has no access to socially recognized power. . . . She is a female in a society in which the community leaders (including her husband) are male. She is young in a society in which being an "elder" is a rank of community leadership. She is isolated and alone: she is inarticulate . . . vulnerable to sex-

ual attack . . . she is simple—she devises no plan to contest the elders. In other words, the story demonstrates that gender status and socio-economic status cross-cut one another; wealth does not ameliorate women's subordination.[7]

Not only is she viewed as one more casualty in the gender war, Susanna is given a victory over her oppressors by contrasting her structural lack of strength and power with her strength and power of spirit. This particular form of critique of Susanna provides a much more sociological and theological analysis of her story. The cultural hermeneutic that falls out of this commentary broadens the scope of criticism of the scripture.

"Yet our argument is not that Susanna has no strength. Our argument is that she has no structural strength. . . . She has moral strength which defeats structural strength."[8]

The feminist argument goes further, critiquing her situation as having a unique outcome, but one that makes her dependent on a male. Whether this unique situation comes from her spiritual or moral strength is not made clear by this particular commentary, as is evident in the following quote:

> Significantly, other biblical women do not escape rape: Dinah, the concubine at Gibeah, Tamar. Only Susanna escapes rape, though through no power of her own. In other words, if a biblical man chooses to rape a woman there are only two possible endings to the story: she is raped or a wise saintly man saves her, but she is not allowed to save herself. . . . The Israelite attitude about rape is spelled out in the Pentateuch. If a virgin were raped outside the city walls, the rapist was ordered to pay the woman's father compensation (bride price) and the two were ordered to marry (Deut. 22:28–29) and if the rape victim belonged to an enemy group . . . rape was treated as a legitimate way for men to breed slaves or acquire concubines.[9]

From much different perspective—art, culture, religion, and gender, Susanna has inspired and challenged a diverse audience. A major question still remains to be answered—that is, how does Susanna fit into our understanding of God's unfolding plan for salvation?

JUSTICE READING STRATEGY

Contemporary churches have found new uses for the story of Susanna. Many of them use the story as an opportunity to look at issues of corruption, sexual harassment, and immorality in the church and especially among the clergy. It is indeed a story that has relevance to women today, who are trapped by powerlessness in some aspects of their culture. When using the justice reading strategy, the reader can view Susanna as one who surely has a place in God's plan for salvation. One of the important lessons to be learned from the narrative is the courage and faithfulness of Susanna in a time of trial. She exhibits rare and raw spiritual power, knowingly and willingly, in the midst of structural power.

She is the paramount example of a Jew who maintains faith and hope in God during the Babylonian exile. Susanna's clarion call for God to come into the midst of her dilemma and deliver her from injustice gives her a position in scripture that few women occupy. She is a woman of courage and commitment, a woman of faith and obedience. When she calls out to God, the scripture tells us that she is heard. While Daniel may have been the human deliverer of Susanna, it is God who provides the freedom. Susanna is a paragon of spiritual power—spiritual power that exist for those whom society cannot and does not protect. Like Hagar before her, God hears her cry and delivers her from death.

Like Vashti, Susanna refused to succumb to the demands of humans, but rather resisted personal debasement and opted for dignity and a chance at salvation. It is not lost on the reader that Daniel in his accusations of the elders tells one that in the past he had been able to intimidate women to go along with his lustful desires because of their fear. "This is how you have been treating the daughters of Israel, and they were intimate with you through fear; but a daughter of Judah would not tolerate your wickedness" (v. 57).

Susanna was able to say "no," just as Vashti had said "no." Susanna, however, is described as going a step further. In Vashti, we just hear the narrator tell us about her refusal of the king; however, Susanna chooses not to obey the men. "Susanna groaned and said, 'I am completely trapped. For if I do this, it will mean death for me; if I do not, I cannot escape your hands. I choose not to do it; I will fall into your hands, rather than sin in the sight of the Lord.'" (vv. 22–23).

The choice creates a strong sense of personal righteousness that is pleasing to God. Susanna, according to the justice reading strategy, instructs now as before about how God wants us to respond to the human power that is proven to be no match for the divine power of God. Into God's hands Susanna put her fate, and God delivered her from the throes of death.

This story of defiance and resistance speaks across the ages to women and men who take their fear in the potential for humans to do harm and place that fear where it should be—as fear of God, which is truly the beginning of wisdom. Daniel may have been given the opportunity to exhibit wisdom during his trial of the elders, but the narrative begins by telling us that Susanna is indeed wise, because she is described as one who feared God, which according to the Proverbs is the beginning of wisdom. There is little question that she is part of God's salvific plan. Her actions should not be categorized as the feminist writers did—as one who was delivered by a man out of a situation of danger. Her deliverance came from God, in whom she had the utmost faith and obedience. Megan McKenna describes her as follows: "Susanna and her relationship with the Holy One are the focuses of the story. She who fears God, loves much."[10]

A WORLD SAYS "NO" TO ZINA IN NIGERIA AND PAKISTAN

Zina is a term in Islam that is used to refer to a woman who has committed adultery or voluntary sexual intercourse outside of marriage. The man involved in the act can deny his role and not be punished, but the woman can be charged on the witness of one person. Unless there are four witnesses to the actions of the man, he is not punished for adultery. As Western women battle sexual harassment on the job and in public places, women in other countries must contend with situations not unlike that of Susanna. Two stories in the early years of this century shed some light on the issue of the cultural and structural powerlessness of women regarding issues of sexuality and adultery. These women in Pakistan and Nigeria are controlled by men in authority whose words and witness can mean life and death to them with or without a fair trial.

Pakistan

Newsweek, the weekly news magazine, in the summer of 2002 reported on a story about an incident in a small village in Pakistan that made international headlines.

> In June, three men in the village of Meerwala accused an 11-year-old boy of an affair with their 30-year-old sister. As punishment for the boy's supposed offense, a tribal council decreed that the men should gang rape his sister Mia, a teacher. The sentence was carried out in front of 500 witnesses. Authorities later determined that the three men had invented the accusation to cover up their own rape and sodomy of the boy.[11]

Unfortunately for these men, the spotlight had been placed on Pakistan because of its military significance to the United States following the war in Afghanistan (2001–2003). That war and the turnaround in leadership that provided more freedom for Afghanistan women also shed light on the cultural practices of Pakistan. The foreign media began reporting on the story and the authorities were forced to punish the men. Had it not been for the worldwide attention, their fate would have been different—it may have gone unnoticed by the world.

Nigeria

The role of women in many twenty-first-century cultures continues to be one of oppression and murder for perceived or real adultery. For most it is a death sentence. Pakistan is not alone in this practice. Zina occurs in others countries as well. Nigeria is one.

In the same summer of the gang rape in Pakistan, an Islamic court in Nigeria sentenced a single mother to death by stoning for having sex outside of marriage. The international spotlight once again pierced the veil of culture and allowed a larger audience to look in.

This time human rights advocates such as Amnesty International and the National Organization for Women, other organizations, and governments of the West condemned the actions of the courts, appealed to the president of Nigeria, and demanded action from the U.S. State Department to prevent Nigeria from executing thirty-year-old Amina Lawal.

The United States, Britain, Sweden, the European Union, Spain, and Italy sent letters of protest to Nigeria. "I'm very upset that a woman is sentenced to stoning in the year 2002," the foreign minister of Sweden is quoted as saying.[12]

The *Rocky Mountain News* editorial described the sentence of Lawal in this way:

> An Islamic court in the town Fanua found Amina Lawal, 30, guilty of having sex out of wedlock, the penalty for which is to be half buried in the ground and then stoned to death. All the proof the court needed was that Lawal had a child more than nine months after divorce. In what the court seemed to think was an act of generosity and mercy, it has delayed the execution until Lawal's baby is weaned.[13]

Lawal's sentence followed an earlier case in which an appeals court acquitted the woman. The Islamic high court, however, upheld the decision of the lower court in Lawal's case.

CONCLUSION

As is evident from these two examples, the story of Susanna resonates with women around the world, even today. With women in the West it usually translates into looking at sexual harassment and being in a situation where power is used to coerce women into sexual relationships. Whether on the job or in a social situation, power is the basis for many men, and at times women, to gain control over another for the purposes of sexual intercourse.

When we look at the story of Susanna, we see in it God using a woman of faith to remind an unfaithful remnant of Israel—separated by the exile, and in some instances lost in alien cultures—that God still hears their cries and responds to their needs. Susanna's words are powerful when she responds to the elders. She says that she would rather disobey them than to disobey God. God's people need to know that they can be faithful even in times of danger and potential death. God's people need to know that when they cry out God's spirit will become an advocate, an intercessor, a paraclete for them. That was what Daniel was sent to do for Susanna. The Holy Spirit that became flesh in Jesus and was named, claimed, and left behind for those who believe is a clear presence for all to partake of.

Susanna becomes a heroine who gains her strength and her steadfastness at a time when the Israelites thought that they no longer had a connection with God. God proved available and present for them. As we peer in on cultures globally, we recognize that we must, with the help of the Holy Spirit, call for and demand humane and fair trials for women who are locked into cultures and traditions that render them powerless over their bodies. How is the Spirit working through those of us who know the story of Susanna and who believe that spiritual power can overcome destructive cultural power in order to exact justice? This is the challenge facing anyone who reads the story of Susanna and follows the inhumane treatment of women throughout the world.

Even though Susanna has a message to convey to contemporary Western women as they continue to fight various forms of sexual harassment with legal and structural changes, women in developing countries suffer at a more basic level, with very little legal or cultural redress. It would be arrogant and shallow to claim the story of Susanna as a paradigm for women in Western cultures, without taking into account that the majority of the women in the world continue to suffer at the hands of corrupt governments and cultural and religious traditions that prevent them from attaining human justice. But their situations do not place them outside the arc of protection of divine justice. For many of them, divine justice is sometimes their only hope. This scripture speaks to these women loudly and clearly—that their spiritual power outweighs their structural and cultural powerlessness because God hears their cries.

THEOLOGICAL REFLECTION AND QUESTIONS

1. The elders were using their power to attempt to persuade Susanna to commit adultery with them. How does this compare to the issues of sexual harassment and rape in situations where there is a disproportionate level of power between men and women? Discuss.

2. Why do you believe that the narrative never speaks about anyone standing up on behalf of Susanna—such as her husband, relatives, or friends—to say that she is innocent? Why is it that no one challenged the elders?

3. How would you use this story to develop a workshop on sexual harassment?

4. Susanna is said to have looked toward "heaven" when she resolved not to sleep with the elders and the elders are said to have "turned their eyes away from heaven when they plotted to seduce her." Discuss the manner in which these two phrases are used in this story.

5. How would you design a justice and witness ministry to support women in developing countries that still maintain tribal practices that are destructive to the lives of women?

6

The Anointing at Bethany

A Woman's Prophetic Act

SCRIPTURE READINGS
Mark 14:3–9; Matthew 26:6–13; John 12:1–8
Also read for comparison: Luke 7:36–50

There are two instances within scripture where attempts are made to anoint Jesus with oil. One attempt succeeded, the other failed. Both were by women. This first attempt is by a woman who is nameless in one account, but called Mary in another. The unsuccessful attempt comes after the crucifixion, as the Marys go to the tomb to anoint Jesus' body and discover that it is no longer there. Both of the scenes describe women who come bearing spices for the anointing. Anointing the body before burial using spices and oil was a custom in the Jewish tradition (2 Chron. 16:14). Anointing a body before death was a ritual of prophecy associated with the proclaiming of a Messiah (Jer. 34:5). Thus, the anointing of Jesus was a prophetic act performed by the woman who silently walked into a room full of hostile disciples and proceeded to anoint Jesus, signifying his role as the Messiah.

There are several questions that come to mind when reading this scripture. The first is what was the rationale behind Christ's self-indulgence with the woman anointing him in lieu of providing for the poor? Was Christ making a statement about the poor that went against his teachings? How has the woman, who is a stranger, been able to accept the idea of service to the Messiah when the disciples have more from which to draw, but still are not able to grasp the significance of his presence? Why is this woman, like so many others in the New Testament, given significance in terms of faithfulness and acceptance of the Messiah, but yet consistently referred to as a minor (nameless) figure, even as she becomes pivotal in God's plan? Was Jesus transitioning from his fully human self to his fully divine self, as some biblical scholars believe?

This scripture raises a number of questions that continue to be studied and analyzed by scholars, preachers, and church leaders. A few churches have come to recognize that this story of the anointing of Jesus is the gateway to the Passion narrative. Other churches still leave this story out of the Passion Week liturgy. Whether this scripture is included in the Passion narrative or not, it is clear that the woman's entrance into the room with the disciples marks a pivotal point in the gospel and has its own theological significance. Jesus no longer speaks of his ministry, but of his messianic mission. Jesus is impatient with the disciples in their response to her presence. He is eager to let them know that a change is about to take place and her actions are a part of that change to come. He says that her act should be remembered wherever the gospel story is told. Yet, most readers forget her and go forward with the betrayal of Judas, as though he is the most important one to remember. She is indeed the vessel through which the reader discovers the true nature of the Messiah. Her anointing provides a clearer understanding of Jesus' messianic purpose. At a time when Jesus reminds the disciples that his earthly work is nearing completion and it is left to his followers to continue, she appears. "The poor will always be with you," does not imply that Jesus has given up on the poor, but rather that he has turned that over to the rest of his followers. It is a message that the disciples will carry far beyond the day of the anointing.

What is most startling about the action in this passage is that the woman, in her silence, performs a bold act of resistance. By approaching the men and walking past them to get to Jesus, she has already broken with the customs of the day—entering into the room of men. She continues to walk toward Jesus when the complaining disciples "cautioned" Jesus about having her come in. Her economic sacrifice is also evident, in that she provides expensive oil with which to anoint Jesus. Her very presence annoys the disciples.

This chapter will discuss the bold action taken by the woman who entered the room filled with men—the disciples—and anointed Jesus. Her action reflected an act of resistance that caused ridicule from the disciples, but ended with praise from Jesus. It was the prophetic act of this woman that initiates the narrative for the passion story.

RETELLING THE NARRATIVE

In Mark (14:3–9) and Matthew (26:6–13) the story of the anointing of Jesus at Bethany is positioned in between the plot to kill Jesus (Mark 14:1–2; Matt. 26:1–5) and Judas' agreement to betray him (Mark 14:10–11; Matt. 26:14–16). In John the story is placed between the plot to kill Jesus (John 11:45–57) and the plot to kill Lazarus (John 12:9–19). In Mark and Matthew the woman is unnamed, but in John she is described as Mary, the sister of Lazarus. In Mark (14:9) and Matthew (26:13), Jesus tells us that we should "remember her" wherever the story of the good news is proclaimed. In

John, Jesus does not ask that we remember her, but he does acknowledge her actions with approval. Matthew (26:8) actually identifies those present as the disciples; Mark only implies that the disciples are in the room. In Mark (14:3) and Matthew (26:6) the anointing takes place at Bethany in the home of Simon the leper. In John (12:1), the anointing takes place in Bethany, but at the home of Lazarus.

The anointing at Bethany marks the beginning of the Passion story. This entrance of the woman literally opens the door to the Passion narrative. As the disciples recline with Jesus, their mood is disturbed by the presence of this woman. Without saying a word, she walks toward Jesus and begins anointing his head with oil in Mark (14:3) and Matthew (26:7) and his feet in John (12:3). From the Hebrew tradition, we surmise that the anointing in Mark and Matthew is a sign of Jesus' messiahship.

The disciples have knowledge of the custom, but they ignore it and choose to scold the woman instead. Lamenting the fact that the poor could have put the money spent for such extravagant oil to better use, the disciples ridicule her. The disciples just do not understand—Jesus redefines the event as a "good one." He implies that because she has had the foresight to anoint his body for its burial, whenever the good news is proclaimed in the entire world, she should be remembered for such an act. This line has given rise to the characterization of this woman as a prophet in that by her actions she is preparing the way for the recognition of Jesus as the Messiah. His subsequent death and resurrection have been preordained by God.

This story also appears in another form in the Gospel of Luke. In Luke the anointing is connected with a parable about undeserved grace, redemption, and forgiveness. The woman is described as a sinner, one from whom Jesus has cast out demons. The story is not used as a part of the Passion narrative, but rather as another lesson leading up to a teaching about forgiveness and sin. The woman is not a prophetess, but a sinner seeking to benefit from God's grace. For purposes of this book, we will look at the Mark, Matthew, and John narratives because they address the quiet resistance of the woman who performed this prophetic act.

TRADITIONAL COMMENTARY

"Leave her alone." Jesus says these three words in response to Judas's evaluation of Mary's anointing of Jesus' feet with costly perfume and then wiping them with her hair. They are a command from the Master to the disciple who is out of line, who is speaking out of malice, ignorance, or blindness. Even without the context of the story, the words are about freedom and noninterference. And they infer praise; infer allowance for Mary and for her behavior and intentions. These words announce that Mary has been recognized and accepted—and so, defended and protected.[1]

In many commentaries throughout the years, this story was referred to as the "anointing of Jesus"—a scripture with no connection to the ones that bracketed it. Considering it as an integral part of the Passion narrative is a relatively new approach to the scripture. Yet, it is evident from the placement of the story in Mark, Matthew, and John that it has a crucial place in the Passion event. Positioned between the plot against Jesus and his betrayal and arrest, the text punctuates the transition that Jesus makes between his earthly works and his messianic mission. Not only is it evident in her actions, but it is also evident in his words about her. "Let her alone; why do you trouble her? She has performed a good service for me" (Mark 14:6).

Notwithstanding the placement of the scripture and the trend toward considering it as the gateway to the Passion event, popular commentaries have continued to look at it in isolation and not in tandem with the stories before and after it. In *Harper's Bible Commentary,* the narrative is critiqued in isolation—independent from the surrounding text:

The likely independent story of a woman who anoints Jesus . . . recounted at different places in the ministry of Jesus . . . is inserted between the two plots to contrast two attitudes toward the suffering Jesus, betrayal or devotion. The narrative stresses two things, the action of the woman and its interpretation . . . and the defense by Jesus against her detractors.[2]

Harper's does, however, make a critical link between the story of the anointing of Jesus before burial and the women who go to the tomb to anoint him after death. In this respect the scripture is given more significance within the context of the total Passion narrative—in essence negating the earlier criticism that disconnects it from the Passion story. The following quote connects the anointing before Jesus' death and resurrection to the attempted anointing after his resurrection:

Her action creates an arch to the ending of the passion narrative where women accompany Jesus to the cross . . . and again propose to anoint him. . . . the woman's action is praised by Jesus in solemn language (14:9, "Amen I say to you").[3]

The story of the "anointing" can also be critiqued from the point of view of two different translations of the Bible—the King James Version (KJV) and the New Revised Standard Version (NRSV). The King James Version of the Bible has been criticized as being sexist in language and in some instances insensitive to racial connotations. In the case of the anointing at Bethany, the KJV may have contributed to the neglect of this scripture, both in the commentaries and in the church.

There are distinctions between the two interpretations with respect to the nuance of language. Of the instances of linguistic differences, one is a matter of translation, and the other a set of terms that actually shades meaning.

The first is the name used for the ointment. In the NRSV the ointment is referred to as "nard" and in the KJV it is referred to as "spikenard." *The Interpreter's Dictionary of the Bible* gives clarity to the two names as follows:

> Nard . . . (*loan word from* Sanskrit). . . . A costly fragrance ointment prepared from the roots and hairy stems of an aromatic Indian herb, *Nardostactrys jatamansi*. . . . In the OT it appears in the Song of Solomon as a perfume giving fragrance to the king's couch (1:12) and as one of several fragrant spices listed symbolically in praise of the bride (4:13–14). The expression translated "pure nard" in the RSV and "spikenard" in the KJV . . . [4]

There is no distinction between the types of ointment; both agree that it is expensive and that the cost is worthy of note. The reference to the ointment as having been used as a fragrance in seduction is brought up in one of the commentaries to raise a question about its intent. "The ointment was a perfume, not quite an ointment," is the point made in an older commentary, giving rise to the perception that perhaps the woman's intent was not that of an anointing, but rather one that was part of a seduction ritual.[5] It is this type of commentary that hinders us in exploring the texts and its theological significance vis-à-vis its place in the salvation story.

The linguistic distinction that shades the meaning of the two versions involves the companion words that describe the reaction of the disciples in Mark and Matthew. In John the comment is attributed to Judas (12:4). The NRSV refers to the anger (Mark 14:4) of those who criticized the woman for anointing Christ, while the KJV refers to the indignation within themselves (Mark 14:4). In response to these emotions, the KJV describes the disciples as murmuring against her and the NRSV states that they scolded her (Mark 14:5). The implications of these two actions and the response could very well shade the meaning of the texts. Since anger is a stronger response than indignation, it implies a more strident and aggressive reaction on the part of the disciples. Given Mark's view of the disciples, it would appear that indignation speaks more to their character.

Because of the approach by Mark to the Gospel—a rush to the cross—it is not unusual to see that this story is brief and lacks the detail that appears in John and Matthew. Mark does, on the other hand, place the anointing between the plot to kill Jesus and his betrayal and arrest. In Mark's narrative, Jesus takes another opportunity to repeat his reason for coming and dying on the cross. The woman validates his claim about the fate of the Son of Man. The narrative of the woman is used, then, as a means of demonstrating her loyalty to and recognition of his fate while the disciples have yet to make that connection.

With seventy-two verses, this chapter is the longest in Mark. And all of it describes the drama leading up to the crucifixion, which for Mark is the most significant act of the gospel. It could be concluded, then, that the fact that the anointing story is included in this lengthy chapter affirms its place in the Passion narrative.

Although the text captures a distinctive event, the event itself is given its contextual meaning by the surrounding texts. It is necessary to read the entire chapter to give cohesion to the significance of Jesus' words regarding the importance of the anointing. This is unlike in Luke where the text stands alone (7:36–50) without the event of the crucifixion.

There are some differences in the three gospel writers' recording of the event. Mark and Matthew agree that the act took place at a dinner in the home of Simon the leper. John has the anointing taking place at Lazarus' home. The timing only varies when bringing into play John's text, where the event is placed six days before the crucifixion; in Mark and Matthew it occurs two days before the crucifixion.

The location is certain in each case; Bethany is approximately two miles from Jerusalem. Mark 14:3–9 places Jesus, along with his disciples, in Bethany where he is in the home of Simon the leper. The *Interpreter's Dictionary* has described this Simon thus: "Simon, a leper, could possibly be the husband of Martha or the father of Mary, Martha and Lazarus. If he once was a leper, he obviously had been cured of his disease, possibly by Jesus."[6]

In general the situation is implied in Mark that the time is nigh for Jesus to end his earthly ministry, and the anointing highlights this critical point. Jesus is still trying to get the disciples to understand the nature of his messianic mission. In Mark, the disciples are generally depicted as too obtuse to get the point and just as they think they understand, Jesus must once again bring them back to a fuller understanding of his life and the expectations for theirs. The shocking entrance of the woman with her ointment creates the scene for reinforcing Jesus' pronouncements.

From the point of view of Jewish ceremonial timing, this act takes place two days prior to the Passover. Jesus is preparing for the Passover dinner with his disciples. He is also taking the time in this chapter to discuss the betrayal and then to move ahead with trying to prepare the disciples for what will come next.

The text is clearly one that speaks to the eventual unfolding of the plan in Mark. The biblical scholar Jack Dean Kingsbury writes in his book *Conflict in Mark* that Mark's Jesus story is "one of swift action and high drama," leading toward the inevitable Passion story.[7]

Kingsbury goes on to critique the disciples, using this example of the anointing as one that affirms their actions throughout the scripture, by saying, "the disciples are imperceptive, disloyal, deceitful, and apostate."[8] Compared to the woman anointing Jesus, these descriptions of the disciples are harsh. She is viewed as one that is loyal, faithful, and prophetic.

This is done more by Jesus than any interpretation that might come out of the commentaries. Kingsbury views the woman, however, as a "minor" character in the Passion story, even though Jesus gives her a major role in the proclamation of the good news.

The story also points to the disciples' desire for status as opposed to service. Jesus makes no social statement about the poor in his rejection of the disciples' ire. "The focus is the presence of Jesus, not the assertion that poverty is a permanent social problem."[9]

It is at this point that the questions and focus of the scripture begin to evolve into an in-depth look into what the actual action of the woman was in the sight of Jesus. Clearly, from the perspective of Mark, it is part of the overall plan for Christ.

"Jesus perceived sheer beauty in her act and proclaimed it," says Walter Lowrie in his commentary. "Kalon, the word used to describe her action, is translated as beauty, not good."[10]

Feminist commentary on the anointing has also been substantial. In general, it has taken the event as a way of acknowledging that Jesus affirms the existence of women in the ministry as those who can and have carried the gospel. Others see this as a way of getting her story to become a part of the Passion narrative.

Mary Anne Getty-Sullivan shares the latter view:

John definitely is describing events linking the anointing by Mary to the last meal Jesus shared with his disciples. As with the transposition of the meaning of the memorial sharing to Chapter 6, John could have had several reasons for doing this. Perhaps he wanted to "demystify" the Eucharist, to stress its meaning rather than to exaggerate it as a ritual. Jesus is underscoring the meaning of both and the importance of this memory when the disciples gathered as a community.[11]

The *Women's Bible Commentary* states:

> The action has a twofold meaning: Jesus equates it with the rituals that accompany burial (Matthew 26:12) and so acknowledges women's traditional role. But anointing the head is also a sign of a royal commission, and thus the woman is cast here in the untraditional position of priest and/or prophet.[12]

As is evident from these two feminist views of the scripture, the woman who anoints Jesus has gained new meaning for scholars and clergy. It is undoubtedly writings such as these that contribute much to a better understanding of her role in the gospel. Ultimately, however, it is Jesus who gives meaning to her actions—that's good news.

JUSTICE READING STRATEGY

What role does this woman play in God's salvific plan?—a significant one. It would seem that it is obvious that the woman who anointed Jesus before the crucifixion would play an integral part in the salvation story, but as is evident from the commentary, that is an assumption that cannot be taken for granted.

Her actions take the place of the attempt at anointing Jesus' body after his death. As a matter of fact, what Mary and the other women at the tomb could not do because Jesus arose, this woman does because of the anticipation of his resurrection. The anointing of the dead was a custom that the women at the tomb wanted to fulfill, but the woman who anoints Jesus follows another custom. Her actions speak to the future and the nature of the Christ of faith. Her actions form a demarcation between Jesus' early life and work and his heavenly spirit and the work of his followers.

In her nonviolent quiet rebellion, this woman speaks volumes. Jesus gives her the necessary affirmation to let us know that she has a place in God's salvific plan. Her mysterious appearance speaks in large measure to God's providence and her determination and courage to walk before the disciples and go directly to Jesus speaks to her faith. We should remember her because she helped point the way to the Christ of faith, following the life and ministry of the Jesus of history. That she is not remembered reflects more on our inability to embrace all of God's people in the unfolding of the plan for redemption. Of the many quotations of Jesus, these words are not often repeated and quoted: "Truly I tell you, wherever the good news is proclaimed in the whole world, what she has done will be told in remembrance of her" (Mark 14:9).

Clearly, this woman is a part of the overall plan for Christ's gift of salvation. She is surely to be memorialized for her acts, even as Christ had requested that the last supper wine and bread be used "in memory" of him. The ceremonial nature of the sacred anointing, then, was not necessarily a good act that went along with Christ's earthly duties, but perhaps a beautiful act as it relates to the aesthetic of his life and the meaning of that life on earth. Her role in God's salvific plan is clear; her actions are a sign and an affirmation to us that lets us know that Jesus is indeed the Messiah.

WOMEN WHO SAY "YES" TO GOD'S CALL

More than a decade before entering ministry, I produced a public television program entitled "He Never Sent Women: The Ordination of a Female Priest." It was a documentary on the African American Catholic Congregation—a breakaway sect of the Catholic Church. One of the most controversial acts of this church was to ordain a woman priest. The Ordination took place in Philadelphia, at the same church in which seven Episcopal women were ordained in the 1970s without the blessing of the established Episcopal Church in America.

The history of the Episcopal women who were ordained in the early '70s was one of the most publicized acts of resistance in the struggle for women's ordination. Their bold action led them to engage some retired male priests who supported their ordination and acted on it. But the church would not accept their ordination and for almost half a decade, they went unrecognized as priests and shunned by colleagues. Finally, after much struggle, they were accepted. The Episcopal Church has gone on to ordain female bishops. However, even though the greater church has moved on, many congregations and male clergy within the Episcopal Church have not.

In the spring of 2002, a woman bishop on the East coast was successful in her civil lawsuit against a male priest who refused to allow her in his pulpit. The courts found that he had to comply with the church's decision to empower a female bishop to supervise his congregation and him. This struggle continues in various ways in other denominations as well, as women move into ministerial roles.

Producing and writing the show was my first introduction to the controversy surrounding the ordination of women. Little did I know that I would enter the clergy less than half a decade later. It never occurred to me that I would have to face such discrimination. The most blatant that I can recall I recount as follows:

When I read the scripture about the anointing at Bethany, I am reminded of the time when I used it to counter a pastor who was unwelcoming of women in the pulpit. It was at a revival in an African American Baptist church in the Midwest. This church had been a sister church to ours for over thirty years and the pastor was gracious to me as I came on board as the first African American and the first woman to pastor my church. On this particular day, the church, as is true in the Baptist tradition, had a revival and the young man who spoke stirred the place up. I arrived late and sat in the back of the church, until the host pastor called to me to come forward and join the other ministers in the pulpit (all male). As I joined them, I extended my hand to each of the ministers in the pulpit; all but one shook my hand. Following the sermon, the pastor of the church asked for the ministers in the pulpit to say a few words.

The minister who had refused to shake my hand spoke first. He was a retired African American preacher about eighty years old at the time. When he stood to speak, he turned toward the congregation, placed his hand on the Bible and began to talk—"I believe in the Word of God that's in this Bible," he said. "We need more men to preach this word. We need men to say 'thus sayeth the Lord.' We need men to proclaim the gospel," and he added, turning toward me, "We don't need any more of these false prophets."

The noticeably embarrassed host pastor turned to me and asked if I wanted to speak. I began by saying that I felt a little bit like the woman who walked into the midst of the male disciples. I reminded the congregation of this woman and her presence in the room of hostile men, who thought that she should not be there. I reminded them of how gracious Jesus had been to her and how Jesus stood up for her and affirmed her in the midst of that hostility. I thanked the host pastor for being as gracious as Jesus had been.

I took my seat. When the service was over, I reached out my hand once again to the minister who refused to acknowledge me and he turned away.

Women in the pulpit as ministers must continue to witness in a prophetic way, because for many of us that is our calling.

CONCLUSION

The other Gospels connect an anointing of Jesus by a woman to his passion, death, and burial. In Matthew, Mark, and John, the woman acts as a prophet; her anointing is a prophetic recognition of Jesus as Messiah. It ought to be noted that an anointing of Jesus by a woman is one of the few stories that is recorded in all four Gospels. That is one indication of how significant this event was for the evangelists and therefore also for us.[13]

The woman who anoints Jesus at Bethany has been left out of the most critical story of the good news, in spite of the fact that Jesus said that we ought to remember her. Her resistance and her determination to perform this "beautiful" act can be a source of encouragement and strength for women who might be engaging in the struggle for freedom to act on God's call in their lives.

Her prophetic witness might be just the right message for women who, once called, find it difficult to exercise their call in a prophetic ministry. To know that Jesus is on your side protecting you from the hostility of those who would not like you to do God's will is always a source of new-found strength. Her story shakes the disciples and us out of our complacency and into the new reality of what Jesus' life, ministry, death, and resurrection are all about. We should remember her not only for what she did, but also for what she means for those who are called to perform prophetic acts in hostile environments.

THEOLOGICAL REFLECTION AND QUESTIONS

1. Why do you think that many churches skip over or exclude this story from the Passion Week sermons?

2. If you were to write a sermon on the anointing at Bethany, what would your thesis statement be?

3. What role does this woman play in God's salvific plan?

4. How significant do you think this story is in the context of women in the church and in the religious community?

5. Jesus says that she performs a good deed. What do you think he means?

Epilogue

This journey through the Bible looking at and studying women who rebelled against injustice in the furtherance of God's plan for salvation was borne out of a small act of resistance against an attempt at intimidation and misuse of power. The good that comes from this action, however, far outweighed the experience that generated it. What does it mean to partake in everyday acts of resistance for the sake of justice? Sometimes, as in the case of Vashti, it just takes saying "no" when you have had enough of self-imposed oppression. Sometimes, as in the case of Shiprah and Puah, it means introducing your own spiritual ethics into a professional situation and saying "no" to life-denying actions. Other times it may mean that your fear of God outweighs your fear of men and/or women and you respond to God's call on your life despite the consequences, just as Susanne did. Or perhaps, like the woman who anoints Jesus at Bethany, you silently perform an act that furthers an understanding of the gospel message, even when you are in hostile environments. As much as we love our parents and try to honor them, there comes a time when we must say "no" to even their actions if they are contrary to God's unfolding liberating goals.

Saying "no" to injustice in the world is not always easy, but what these stories have shown is that God uses all of God's creation to further the goal of justice in the world. Women and men of faith, courage, and vision can make themselves available for God's purposes. The consequences that arise as a result of the decision to follow God's lead may lead to calamity, but the clarity of conscience that follows is a reward that cannot be purchased.

Even with the biblical story providing sustenance for everyday acts of resistance, the world still harbors injustices against women that require bold and committed men and women to turn around situations that are life denying—barbarous murders committed against women who are accused of adultery; making sex slaves of young girls by fetish priests, coverups of war crimes against women, and the use of girls and women as commodities for settling tribal disputes. All these injustices require global mobilization using large and small acts of resistance to change conditions for women without a voice.

If this book can be used for anything, it should be used as a way to provide awareness and promote action against twenty-first-century injustices against women worldwide. It is also my hope that this book has given the reader another way to interpret the biblical stories. Accepting an inferior position by reading the Bible through the eyes of a victimized person can never result in a wholesome appreciation for the work of God in the world. It was never God's intention to place women in a subordinate or inferior status in creation, but rather embrace the gifts of the totality of God's human creation.

Jesus has the last word on this when he says to the disciples: "Let her alone. Why do you trouble her? She has performed a good service for me. . . . Truly I tell you, wherever the good news is proclaimed in the whole world, what she has done will be told in remembrance of her" (Mark 14:6–9). Whenever we are in doubt about God's call on our lives in times of everyday acts of resistance, we should listen for the voice of Jesus, telling us to "remember her."

Notes

INTRODUCTION

1. Orenthal J. Simpson was accused of murdering his estranged wife, Nicole Brown Simpson. In 1996 a jury comprised primarily of working-class African American women acquitted him.

2. LaVerne M. Gill, *Daughters of Dignity: African Women in the Bible and the Virtues of Black Womanhood* (Cleveland: Pilgrim Press, 2000).

CHAPTER 1

1. Ahasuerus (Hebrew scriptures and NRSV) is referred to as Artaxerxes in the Addition to Esther written in the Greek Apocryphal writings. This book will use the Hebrew version of the story.

2. Jeffrey M. Cohen, "Vashti—an Unsung Heroine," in *Jewish Bible Quarterly* 24 (April–June 1996), 105.

3. Josiah Derby, "The Paradox in the Book of Esther," in *Jewish Bible Quarterly*, 23, no. 2 (April–June, 1995), 116.

4. Bruce M. Metzger and Roland E. Murphy, eds., *The New Oxford Annotated Bible with the Apocryphal/Deuterocanonical Books,* New Revised Standard Version (New York: Oxford University Press, 1994), 613 OT, n. 1.9.

5. René Girard, *Job the Victim of His People,* trans. Yvonne Freccero (Stanford, Calif.: Stanford University Press, 1987), 5.

6. Ibid., 89.

7. Cohen, "Vashti," 105.

8. Ibid., 104.

9. Louis Ginzberg, *The Legends of the Jews, IV: Bible Times and Characters from Joshua to Esther* (Philadelphia: The Jewish Publication Society of America, 1942), 377.

10. Ibid.

11. Ibid., 379.

12. James L. Mays, ed., *Harper's Bible Commentary* (San Francisco: Harper & Row, 1988), 388.

13. Cohen, "Vashti," 106.

14. Rana Dogar, "After a Life of Slavery," *Newsweek,* Atlantic edition, (5 April 1999), 1. www.freetheslaves.net/after_life_of_slavery.htm

CHAPTER 2

1. John Fulton, "A New Chronology—Synopsis of David Rohl's book *A Test of Time*," a debate that appeared on the Hyde Park Christian Fellowship (London: links@debate.org.uk), an informal network of Christian researchers in the UK, whose primary interest is the academic study of all issues relevant to Islam and Christianity.

2. David M. Rohl, *Pharaohs and Kings: A Biblical Quest* (New York: Crown Random House, 1996), 279. This is the U.S. edition of *A Test of Time: The Bible from Myth to History.*

3. Bruce M. Metzger and Roland E. Murphy, eds., *The New Oxford Annotated Bible with the Apocryphal/Deuterocanonical Books,* New Revised Standard Version (New York: Oxford University Press, 1994), 70–71 OT.

4. Everett Fox, *The Schocken Bible, Volume 1: The Five Books of Moses* (New York: Schocken Books, 1995), 250.

5. Fulton, "A New Chronology."

6. Fox, *The Schocken Bible, Vol. 1,* 257–58.

7. Thomas W. Mann, *The Book of the Torah: The Narrative Integrity of the Pentateuch* (Atlanta: John Knox Press, 1988), 80.

8. J. Cheryl Exum, "You Shall Let Every Daughter Live: The Study of Exodus 1:8–2:10," in *Semeia* 28 (1983), 63

9. Fox, *The Schocken Bible, Vol. 1,* 259.

10. Ibid.

11. Ibid., 258.

12. P. Kyle McCarter Jr., "Exodus," in *Harper's Bible Commentary,* ed. James L. Mays (San Francisco: Harper & Row, 1988), 133.

13. Drorah O'Donnell Setel, "Exodus," in *The Women's Bible Commentary,* ed. Carol A. Newsom and Sharon H. Ringe (Louisville: Westminster John Knox Press, 1992), 30.

14. Ibid.

15. Rohl, *Pharoahs and Kings,* 255.

16. Claudia Camp, *Wise, Strange and Holy: The Strange Woman and the Making of the Bible* (Sheffield, England: Sheffield Academic Press, 2000), 237.

17. Mays, *Harper's Bible Commentary,* 191.

18. Camp, *Wise, Strange, and Holy,* 230–31.

19. Mays, *Harper's Bible Commentary,* 146.

20. Metzger and Murphy, *New Oxford Annotated Bible,* 71 OT.

21. Fulton, "A New Chronology."

22. Mark William Olson, "Break Free and Follow," in *The Other Side Online,* (July–August 2000), www.theotherside.org/archive/jul-aug00/olson.html.

23. Darlene Clark Hine, Elsa Barkley Brown, and Rosalyn Terborg-Penn, eds., *Black Women in America: An Historical Encyclopedia,* volume II (Indianapolis: Indiana University Press, 1993), 1243.

24. Ibid.

25. John Hope Franklin and August Meier, eds., *Black Leaders of the Twentieth Century* (Chicago: University of Illinois Press, 1982), 48.

26. René Girard, *Job the Victim of His People,* trans. Yvonne Freccero (Stanford, Calif.: Stanford University Press, 1987), 52.

CHAPTER 3

1. Walter Brueggemann, "First and Second Samuel," in *Interpretation: A Bible Commentary for Teaching and Preaching,* ed. James L. Mays, Patrick D. Miller, and Paul Achtemeier (Louisville: John Knox Press, 1990), 143.

2. Ibid.

3. Jo Ann Hackett, "1 and 2 Samuel," in *The Women's Bible Commentary,* ed. Carol A. Newsom and Sharon H. Ringe (Louisville: Westminster John Knox Press, 1992), 91.

4. Ibid.

5. Ibid.

6. Robert L. Cohn, "1 Samuel," in *Harper's Bible Commentary,* ed. James L. Mays (San Francisco: Harper & Row, 1988) 281.

7. David M. Gunn, "2 Samuel," in *Harper's Bible Commentary,* ed. James L. Mays (San Francisco: Harper & Row, 1988), 292.

8. George Arthur Buttrick, ed., *The Interpreter's Dictionary of the Bible* (Nashville: Abingdon Press, 1996), 251–52.

9. Brueggemann, "First and Second Samuel," 144.

10. Karen Parker, "War Rape," presented to the United Nations Commission on Human Rights, fifty-first session, agenda item 11, 1995.

11. Dottie Horn, "Comfort Women," *Endeavors Magazine,* vol. 13, no. 2 (January 1997). http://research.unc.edu/endeavors/win97/comfort.html

12. Karen Parker, "War Rape."

13. Rod Nordland, "Of Tribes, Trials and Tribulations," *Newsweek,* vol. CXL, no. 6 (5 August 2002), 36.

CHAPTER 4

1. Katharine Doob Sakenfeld, "Journey with God: A Commentary on the Book of Numbers," in *The International Theological Commentary: Bible: O.T. Numbers Commentaries* (Grand Rapids: William B. Eerdmans,

1995), 149.

2. Ibid., 187–88.

3. Walters Riggans, *Numbers* (Philadelphia: Westminister Press, 1983) 199.

4. Kenneth Barker, ed., *The NIV Study Bible* (Grand Rapids: Zondervan Publishing, 1995), 88.

5. Katharine Doob Sakenfeld, "Numbers: Inheritance and Land Distribution," in *The Women's Bible Commentary*, ed. Carol A. Newsom and Sharon H. Ringe (Louisville: Westminster John Knox Press, 1992), 46.

6. Danna Nolan Fewell, "Joshua: Commentary," in *The Women's Bible Commentary*, ed. Carol A. Newsom and Sharon H. Ringe (Louisville: Westminster John Knox Press, 1992), 65.

7. Dennis T. Olson, "Numbers," in *Interpretation: A Bible Commentary for Teaching and Preaching*, ed. James Luther Mays, Patrick D. Miller, and Paul J. Achtemeier, (Louisville: John Knox Press, 1990) 165.

8. Ibid., 166–67.

9. Thomas W. Mann, *The Book of the Torah: The Narrative Integrity of the Pentateuch* (Atlanta: John Knox Press, 1988), 141–42.

10. James L. Mays, ed., *Harper's Bible Commentary* (San Francisco: Harper & Row, 1988), 203.

11. Carol A. Newsom and Sharon H. Ringe, ed., *The Women's Bible Commentary* (Louisville: Westminster John Knox Press, 1992), 50.

12. Olson, "Numbers," 164.

13. Testimony of Mrs. Esther Esimajete, a fisherwoman at Escravos before the Environmental Rights Action (ERA), 12 January 2000. Environmental Testimonies #16, "The Environmental Refugees of Escravos," field report no. 50. www.essentialaction.org/shell/era/escravos.html

14. Testimony of Mrs. Oluch of Escravos before the ERA, 12 January 2000. www.essentialaction.org/shell/era/escravos.html

CHAPTER 5

1. G. S. Wegener, *6000 Years of the Bible* (New York: Harper & Row, 1963), 162–68.

2. Bruce Metzger and Roland E. Murphy, eds., *The New Oxford Annotated Bible with the Apocryphal/Deuterocanonical Books* (New York: Oxford University Press, 1994), 179.

3. Gita Sereny, *Into That Darkness: An Examination of Conscience*

(New York: Vintage, 1983), 99–100.

4. M. Lindsay Kaplan, "Sexual Slander and the Politics of the Erotic in Garter's Susanna," in *The Judgment of Susanna: Authority and Witness,* ed. Ellen Spolsky (Atlanta: Scholars Press, 1996), 73.

5. Sharon Deykin Baris, "Hosannas to an American Susanna," in *The Judgment of Susanna: Authority and Witness,* ed. Ellen Spolsky (Atlanta: Scholars Press, 1996), 119.

6. Ibid., 121, 123.

7. Susan Sered and Samuel Cooper, "Sexuality and Social Control: Anthropological Reflections on the Book of Susanna," in *The Judgment of Susanna: Authority and Witness,* ed. Ellen Spolsky (Atlanta: Scholars Press, 1996), 43–44.

8. Ibid., 45.

9. Ibid., 49–50.

10. Megan McKenna, *Leave Her Alone* (Maryknoll, N.Y.: Orbis Books, 2000), 75.

11. Rod Nordland, "Of Tribes, Trials and Tribulations," *Newsweek,* vol. CXL, no. 6 (5 August 2002), 36.

12. Gilbert DaCosta, "Nigerian Government Silent Despite Pressure to Reverse Death by Stoning Sentence," *Associated Press,* world, general news, 28 August 2002. http://www.Santegidio.org/p&m/news2002/22 _08_02_c.htm

13. "The Savagery of Islamic Law," editorial, 26 August 2002, www. RockyMountainNews.com/archives/opinion/commentary/editorial/34a.

CHAPTER 6

1. Megan McKenna, *Leave Her Alone* (Maryknoll, N.Y.: Orbis Books, 2000), 11.

2. John R. Donahue, "Mark," in *Harper's Bible Commentary,* ed. James L. Mays (San Francisco: Harper & Row, 1988), 1004.

3. Ibid.

4. George Arthur Buttrick, ed., *The Interpreter's Dictionary of the Bible* (Nashville: Abingdon Press, 1996), 510.

5. Albert Barnes, *Notes on the New Testament: Matthew and Mark* (Grand Rapids: Baker Book House, 1884), 381.

6. Buttrick, *Interpreter's Dictionary,* 357.

7. Jack Dean Kingsbury, *Conflict in Mark: Jesus, Authorities, Disciples* (Minneapolis: Fortress Press, 1975), 1.

8. Ibid. 13.

9. Raymond E. Brown, S.S.; Joseph A. Fitzmeyer, S.J.; and Roland E. Murphy, O. Carm., eds., *The New Jerome Biblical Commentary* (Englewood Cliffs, N.J.: Prentice Hall, 1990), 625.

10. Walter Lowrie, *Jesus: According to St. Mark* (London: Longman's Green and Company, 1929), 484.

11. Mary Ann Getty-Sullivan, *Women in the New Testament* (Collegeville, Minn.: Liturgical Press, 2001), 218–19.

12. Carol A. Newsom and Sharon Ringe, eds., *The Women's Bible Commentary* (Louisville: Westminster John Knox Press, 1992), 261.

13. Getty-Sullivan, *Women in the New Testament,* 212.

Bibliography

Barker, Kenneth, ed. *The NIV Study Bible.* Grand Rapids: Zondervan Publishing, 1995.

Barnes, Albert. *Notes on the New Testament: Matthew and Mark.* Grand Rapids: Baker Book House, 1884.

Brown, Raymond E., S.S.; Joseph A. Fitzmeyer, S.J.; and Roland E. Murphy, O. Carm., eds., *The New Jerome Biblical Commentary.* Englewood Cliffs, N.J.: Prentice Hall, 1990.

Buttrick, George Arthur, ed. *The Interpreter's Dictionary of the Bible.* Nashville: Abingdon Press, 1996.

Camp, Claudia. *Wise, Strange and Holy: The Strange Woman and the Making of the Bible.* Sheffield, England: Sheffield Academic Press, 2000.

Dagan, Ben Shimon, ed. *The Jewish Bible Quarterly.*

_____. Cohen, Jeffrey M. "Vashti—an Unsung Heroine." Vol. 24, no. 1 (June 1996).

_____. Derby, Josiah. "The Paradox on the Book of Esther." Vol. 23, no. 2 (April–June 1995).

Environmental Rights Action (ERA). 12 January 2000. Environment testimonies #16, "The Environmental Refugees of Escravos." Field report no. 50, testimony of Mrs. Esther Esimajete.

Exum, J. Cheryl. "You Shall Let Every Daughter Live: The Study of Exodus 1:8–2:10. *Semeia.* Volume 28 (1983).

Fox, Everett. *The Schocken Bible, Volume 1: The Five Books of Moses.* New York: Schocken Books, 1995.

Franklin, John Hope, and August Meier, eds. *Black Leaders of the Twentieth Century.* Chicago: University of Illinois Press, 1982.

Fulton, John. "A New Chronology—Synopsis of David Rohl's book, *A Test of Time.*" Hyde Park Christian Fellowship. London: links@debate.org.uk.

Getty-Sullivan, Mary Ann. *Women in the New Testament.* Collegeville, Minn.: Liturgical Press, 2001.

Ginzberg, Louis. *The Legends of the Jews, IV: Bible Times and Characters from Joshua to Esther.* Philadelphia: The Jewish Publication Society of America, 1942.

Girard, René. *Job the Victim of His People.* Trans. Yvonne Freccero. Stanford, Calif.: Stanford University Press, 1987.

Hine, Darlene Clark, Elsa Barkley Brown, and Rosalyn Terborg-Penn, eds. *Black Women in America: An Historical Encyclopedia.* Volume II. Indianapolis: Indiana University Press, 1993.

Kingsbury, Jack Dean. *Conflict in Mark: Jesus, Authorities, Disciples.* Minneapolis: Fortress Press, 1975.

Lowrie, Walter. *Jesus: According to St. Mark.* London: Longman's Green and Company, 1929.

Mann, Thomas. *The Book of the Torah: The Narrative Integrity of the Pentateuch.* Atlanta: John Knox Press, 1988.

Mays, James L., ed. *Harper's Bible Commentary.* San Francisco: Harper & Row, 1988.

_____. Cohn, Robert L. "1 Samuel."

_____. Collins, John G. "Introduction to the Apocrypha."

_____. Donahue, John R. "Mark."

_____. Gunn, David. M. "2 Samuel."

_____. McCarter, P. Kyle., Jr. "Exodus."

Mays, James, L.; Patrick D. Miller; and Paul Achtemeier, eds. *Interpretation: A Bible Commentary for Teaching and Preaching.* Louisville: John Knox Press, 1990.

_____. Brueggemann, Walter. "First and Second Samuel."

_____. Olson, Dennis T. "Numbers."

McKenna, Megan. *Leave Her Alone.* Maryknoll, N.Y.: Orbis Books, 2000.

Metzger, Bruce, and Roland E. Murphy, eds. *The New Oxford Annotated Bible with the Apocryphal/Deuterocanonical Books.* New York: Oxford University Press. 1994.

Newsom, Carol A., and Sharon H. Ringe, eds. *The Women's Bible Commentary.* Louisville: Westminster John Knox Press, 1992.

_____. Fewell, Danna Nolan. "Joshua: Commentary."

_____. Hackett, Jo Ann. "1 and 2 Samuel."

_____. Sakenfeld, Katharine Doob. "Numbers: Inheritance and Land Distribution."

_____. Setel, Drorah O'Donnell. "Exodus."

Nordland, Rod. "Of Tribes, Trials and Tribulations." *Newsweek,* vol. CXL, no. 6 (5 August 2002), 36.

Olson, Mark William. "Break Free and Follow." *The Other Side Online.* July–August 2000. www.theotherside.org/archive/jul-aug00/olson.html.

Riggans, Walter. *Numbers.* Philadelphia: Westminster Press, 1983.

Rohl, David M. *Pharaohs and Kings: A BiblicalQuest.* New York: Crown/Random House, 1996. U.S. edition of *A Test of Time: The Bible from Myth to History.*

Sakenfeld, Katharine Doob. "Journey with God: A Commentary on the Book of Numbers," in *The International Theological Commentary: Bible: O.T. Numbers Commentaries*. Grand Rapids: William B. Eerdmans, 1995.

Sereny, Gita. *Into that Darkness: An Examination of Conscience*. New York: Vintage, 1983.

Spolsky, Ellen., ed. *The Judgment of Susanna: Authority and Witness*. Atlanta: Scholars Press, 1996.

_____. Baris, Sharon Deykin. "Hosannas to an American Susanna."

_____. Kaplan, M. Lindsay. "Sexual Slander and the Politics of the Erotic in Garter's Susanna."

_____. Sered, Susan, and Samuel Cooper. "Sexuality and Social Control: Anthropological Reflections on the Book of Susanna."

Wegener, G. S. *6000 Years of the Bible*. New York: Harper & Row, 1963.

Other books from The Pilgrim Press

DAUGHTERS OF DIGNITY
African Women of the Bible and the Virtues of Black Womanhood
LAVERNE MCCAIN GILL

Exploring theological and historical foundations and tracing the experiences of African women in the Bible, this book is useful for mentoring programs and nurturing. It offers deep ethical and moral heritage illustrations and contains stories of pioneers such as Fannie Lou Hamer, Rosa Parks, and Sojourner Truth.

ISBN 0-8298-1373-X/paper/176 pages/$17.00

MY MOTHER PRAYED FOR ME
Faith Journaling for African American Women
LAVERNE MCCAIN GILL

Gill provides guidance to African American women for writing and recording their spiritual witness. She begins by offering a five-step process for journaling, focusing on stories of the Bible and personal witnesses to the presence of God in contemporary life.

ISBN 0-8298-1396-9/cloth/104 pages/$14.95

INTRODUCING AFRICAN WOMEN'S THEOLOGY
Introductions in Feminist Theology
MERCY AMBA ODUYOYE

Illustrations of African culture and its multireligious context have influenced African Christian women's selection of theological issues.

ISBN 0-8298-1423-X/paper/144 pages/$17.00

DEAR SISTERS
A Womanist Practice of Hospitality

N. LYNNE WESTFIELD
Exploring the "concealed gatherings" used by African American women as a source of fostering resilience, the author explores the larger Christian tradition of hospitality.

ISBN 0-8298-1449-3/paper/144 pages/$17.00

NOT WITHOUT A STRUGGLE
Leadership Development for African American Women in Ministry

BISHOP VASHTI MURPHY MCKENZIE
In this historical, theological, and biblical overview of female leadership in the church, the author suggests a model based on the "Women Surviving in Ministry" project promoting learning and dialogue among peers and mentors.

ISBN 0-8298-1076-5/paper/144 pages/$15.95

To order these or any other books from The Pilgrim Press call or write to:

THE PILGRIM PRESS
700 PROSPECT AVENUE EAST
CLEVELAND, OHIO 44115-1100

Phone orders 1-800-537-3394 ▪ *Fax orders* 216-736-2206

Please include shipping charges of $4.00 for the first book and $0.75 for each additional book. Or order from our web sites at www.pilgrimpress.com and www.ucpress.com.

Prices subject to change without notice.